DISTANCE RIDING
From Start to Finish

DISTANCE RIDING
From Start to Finish

Virginia Weisel Johnson
and Thula Johnson

ILLUSTRATED WITH PHOTOGRAPHS AND DRAWINGS

Houghton Mifflin Company Boston

Library of Congress Cataloging in Publication Data
Johnson, Virginia Weisel.
  Distance riding, from start to finish.
  Bibliography: p.
  Includes index.
  1. Trail riding—Competitions.   2. Endurance riding (Horsemanship)   I. Johnson, Thula, joint author.   II. Title.
SF296.T7J63   798'.23   76-21287
ISBN 0-395-24773-X

Printed in the United States of America

V 10 9 8 7 6 5 4 3 2

TO MARGIT SIGRAY BESSENYEY

"Riding consists of control over yourself and respect for the horse."

Karl Friedrich von Langen,
German Olympic Gold Medalist

Acknowledgments

IT WOULD BE impossible to thank all the people and the horses who contributed to this book but we would like to name a few persons whose help was particularly appreciated; Mr. Henry B. Davis, Curator, United States Cavalry Museum, Fort Riley, Kansas; Mr. Scott Simpson, Montana State University, Bozeman, Montana; Mr. Alexander Mackay-Smith, editor of the *Chronicle of the Horse;* Mrs. Joan Throgmorton, Secretary of the North American Trail Ride Conference, Gilroy, California; Drucilla Barner, Auburn, California, Secretary of the Western States Trail Ride (the Tevis); Barbara Le Fevre, St. Cloud, Florida of the Florida Horseman's Association; Dr. D. P. Hatfield, D.V.M., Victor, Montana; Dr. J. K. Ward, D.V.M. Hamilton, Montana; Dr. R. J. Brophy, D.V.M., Hamilton, Montana; Mr. Steven O'Connell, Chairman of the Eastern Competitive Trail Ride Association; many members of the North American Trail Ride Association who donated pictures and information; and last but not least the volunteer helpers, lay judges, riders, veterinarians, and management officials who have done so much to make Competitive and Endurance Riding a truly inspired amateur sport.

Contents

Illustrations

Introduction
by Richard B. Barsaleau, D.V.M.

Distance Riding: From Start to Finish has an optimistic ring to it — and rightly so! Since this introduction is at the start of the book, I must urge the reader to work from this end and proceed to the conclusion. Why? Because I don't want you to miss *any* of the trip!

There are some things that needed to be said about the sports of Endurance and Competitive Trail Riding — and the authors have said them clearly and in an interesting way.

For those of us who consider Trail Riding as a most natural and enjoyable use of the horse, there is little to say, except: Get out and use your horse *naturally* on terrain that tests the *skills* of the rider and the *condition* of the horse. You will both be the better for it!

And those who prefer to hang their hat in one or the other camp, i.e., Competitive Riding or Endurance Riding, please let me urge you to respond to the enthusiasm of Virginia and Thula Johnson who, without criticism, indicate that both sports indeed have many similarities.

For me, the belief exists that many of our modern-day endurance riders would have greatly benefited had they begun their trail riding competition with the Competitive Trail group. This observation comes from viewing those qualities of *horsemastership* which emerge from the philosophies of such organizations as NATRC and Rocky Mountain Conference, so aptly described by the authors in this informative book.

Finally, after you have read (and re-read) this book, my sincere hope is that some of the experiences detailed for you herein may be put to work for you to assist in your trail riding pleasure. And, I might add, also assist in your *success* as a *competition rider* in either of the two areas of trail riding events.

May your horse always walk *hard* — and trot *easy!* and be looking for

more travel on the day *after* the competition! Then you will have done
some of the right things with and for your horse as presented by Virginia
and Thula Johnson in this excellent, thought-provoking book.

See you on the trails!!

DISTANCE RIDING
From Start to Finish

1. In Distance Riding, We Discover a New World

WE WERE so far behind that we had not seen our fellow competitors for some time although their horses' prints showed they could not be many miles ahead on the trail, which clung precariously to the ridge. The trail was studded with rocks, barred by fallen logs, and wet with melting snow, for we were near timberline. Through the stunted firs we glimpsed the grey stone of the Tetons, and on the mountain below, the trail that we had climbed to the ridge, zig-zagging through scarlet paintbrush, purple lupine and cream-colored columbine.

Ahead of me, my companion urged her horse across a creek and up a steep slope. My Appaloosa mare, aptly named Voodoo, waded into the knee-high torrent, the current shoving her downstream, the rocks turning beneath her feet. Halfway across she tugged at the reins, but I did not dare let her gulp the icy water; she was sweating from the steep climb, and too much to drink could give her colic.

As I pressed Voodoo up the slope, I could see to my rear the two drag riders in their big hats and chaps, spurring their horses around the final zigzag before the trail crossed the creek. Their presence showed that my companion and I were the last competitors, but we had been the last to start in the lightweight division, which numbered twelve entries. Altogether, there were thirty riders, not many compared to Competitive Rides in other parts of the country; but the Jackson Hole Ride was tough, and this was the first one that had been held in the area.

The trail on the other side of the creek had been nearly obliterated by the rain of the previous night, and churned into slippery clay by the riders ahead of us. As she lunged to the top of the slope, Voodoo's hind feet went from beneath her. Frantically she fought to regain her balance. I thought, this is it — over and over, a hundred feet to the boulders in the bottom of the canyon. Paralyzed, I could not move. Thank God I couldn't, or the mare might never have regained her balance. With a last frantic effort she scrabbled back onto the trail, her sides heaving, shook herself crossly, and started off again. She did not like another horse to get too far ahead of her, and my companion was out of sight. I understood perfectly. During the months of training for the Ride, Voodoo and I had learned each other's eccentricities and compromised with mutual understanding.

Behind me, a drag rider called, grinning, "Kinda slippery, ain't it?"

Pretending a nonchalance that I did not feel, I called back, "It sure is!"

I couldn't say anything else, for Voodoo had swung into an extended trot along the trail that crumbled from the side of the mountain, although it seemed to me that her stride was not as free as before, and I worried that she might have hurt her back, already weakened from her racing days. Out of the clearing and down into a timbered gulch. More rocks. Voodoo stumbled and tried to go on, limping. My heart leaped into my throat as I pulled the mare to a stop and fell out of the saddle. Picking up Voodoo's near foreleg, I examined the foot. There was nothing in the shoe, but when I pressed the sole, the mare winced and tried to pull her leg away. A stone bruise or fault in the shoeing? Or an injury in Arizona before I had bought her? I'd been worried about her feet, as I had about her back, ever since I'd begun conditioning her for the Ride. Her hooves were thin and brittle. The drag riders must have stopped to rest; I couldn't see them, and I couldn't see my companion, who was ahead of me. Remounting, I picked up the reins, whereupon Voodoo immediately started off. Did she limp? I wasn't sure.

How much farther was it to the finish? There was no veterinary check before then, and I did not know if Voodoo was in condition to continue. Would she give up if she didn't feel fit? She was a selfish, temperamental creature, a registered Appaloosa, but mostly Thoroughbred, which explained her racing. I'd bought her in Arizona and trailered her two thousand miles north for competitive trail riding.

In my concern for Voodoo, I was only dimly aware of my own exhaustion. I'd been up since four o'clock — feeding, grooming, saddling; boiling coffee in the camper, with fingers stiff with cold; riding thirty miles across the mountains with ten or fifteen miles still to go within the required time of six and a half to seven hours, which meant no resting or slowing down to a walk except where it was necessary on a steep climb.

I wondered why I hadn't stayed home like a sensible person, instead of riding a horse that might go lame in the wilds of Wyoming. I wasn't even sure I was on the trail, not having seen a red paper plate nailed to a tree for some time. No, there was a plate, and beyond, I glimpsed my companion riding up another zigzag on what looked like a sheer wall of rock.

If I hadn't seen my companion, would I have given up and waited for the drag riders to escort me back to camp? I don't know, because as Voodoo caught sight of the horse ahead of her, she quickened her pace. She wasn't ready to quit.

Some hours later, I thought of that moment on the trail. We had finished the Ride within the required time; Voodoo's pulse and respiration had been taken; the vet had checked her; I had unsaddled, groomed, and fed her; and now I leaned on the bars of her open-air stall. Other horses, similarly confined, were being brushed by their owners or eating. I could smell crushed sagebrush, dust, and horse sweat, and the tang of a wood fire where the cooks were preparing a barbecue. On the far side of the valley, the sunset illuminated the great, lonely peaks of the Tetons. The green meadows below and the river feathered with cottonwood deepened to shadow.

My muscles felt like spaghetti and I was lightheaded with exhaustion. If I could, I would have provided Voodoo with a silver-mounted water bucket. At the finish check, the vet had said that Voodoo had a stone bruise and a sore back, both of which had undoubtedly pained her on the long ride.

"She's got heart, that mare," the vet told me.

I said, "I nearly gave up; she didn't."

I'd remember that always — that a horse had the courage to carry on against great odds. If a horse could do it, why shouldn't I?

"Shoe her with pads," the vet said, "and rest her for a week or so and she'll be all right."

The vet slapped Voodoo's rump, whereupon she directed a wicked look at him from her wall eye. No one could sweet-talk her.

I knew this, and didn't try. As I leaned on the unpeeled fence rail, I thought that it was sufficient to have completed the forty miles. Together, Voodoo and I had accomplished the task we'd set out to do; we'd seen the glory of the mountains and shared the trail with friends. I wouldn't have exchanged places with anyone else in the world.

That is Competitive and Endurance trail riding, one of the fastest growing sports in the United States, and one that is becoming popular in Europe and in Australia.

What are the definitions of these rides? A Competitive Ride is an event in which the contestants cover a certain distance within a required time. If they arrive at the finish too soon, they are penalized, as well as if they arrive too late.

An Endurance Ride is an event in which the contestants cover a given distance with only a maximum time allowance. That is, the rider who comes in first wins. In addition, there is a prize for the horse that arrives in the best time and in the best condition. An Endurance Ride, unlike a Competitive Ride, is a race.

Both events are monitored by judges and veterinarians on the trail to prevent abuse to the horses, and, in both events, horses are checked before being allowed to compete. If, in the opinion of the veterinarians, they are unfit, they are eliminated.

No one checks the rider; he's on his own.

Competitive Riding has only become popular in the last ten years. There were a few rides held annually before that — the Tevis Cup Ride in California and a number of them in the East, such as the Vermont Ride at Woodstock, but few people knew about them. During the first half of the century, the horse, once a necessity for transportation, had become a pleasure animal. The emphasis had turned to showing, where conformation was of paramount importance. Knowledgeable horsemen feared that breeders would sacrifice stamina for what the judges wanted to see in a show ring. A plump, shiny animal might take a blue ribbon, but he could not trot twenty miles on forest trails. The horse, these authorities believed, should be judged for performance, not merely for conformation. The answer was competitive and endurance riding, similar to the military trials the cavalry had held before World War II, monitored so there would be no abuse of the horses. It was not easy to popularize an equestrian event with so little spectator appeal. That this was accomplished was due to the efforts of a few dedicated people. Now the information booklets of the Rides contain this phrase, ". . . The purpose of this Ride is to demonstrate sound methods of conditioning horses . . . and to stimulate interest in horse breeding."

Sharon Saare, the capable chairman of the Appaloosa Horse Club Long Distance Riding Committee, said to me, "It's what a horse can do that's important, not how pretty he is."

Dr. D. P. Hatfield, D.V.M. of Victor, Montana, says, "Competitive trail riding is the last amateur sport left in America."

I could see this at Jackson Hole the morning after we'd done the forty miles, when the prizes were awarded. Contestants, judges, members of the management, the helpers, and a handful of spectators gathered in an aspen grove. Trailers, trucks, and campers were parked in the sagebrush and beneath the shade of pine trees.

"Now, as you know," the chairman of the Jackson Hole Ride observed, "the awards are given to the horse, not the rider. In sixth place, in the heavyweight division — "

A long-legged man, clad in jeans and a big hat, stepped forward with a grin on his face to get his ribbon. He was a millionaire, and the chairman was a part-time blacksmith and rancher; that didn't count. What did was the fact that the man in the heavyweight division had completed the Ride.

In addition to ribbons, the winners of each division and the grand champion won handmade wooden plaques, which did not begin to pay for the expense, time, and trouble of the contestants, but no one objected. Like me, my fellow competitors had won their awards on the trail. No amount of money could buy what we took home in our hearts and memories.

This is a simple explanation of why more and more people are turning to trail riding. It doesn't explain it all, nor why in this day of energy crisis equestrian events in general are attracting so much interest. The Department of Agriculture estimated in 1971 that there were more than 7 million horses in the United States, twice as many as in 1961; and that by 1977 there would be 10 million horses. That is to say that in 1971 there was one horse for every thirty persons, or that in 1977, approximately one person in four would cinch a saddle on a horse once during the year.

When I get up to feed at six o'clock on a winter morning, I'm inclined to agree with friends who say we are crazy. It is cold and dark and I slip on the icy road. At the corral, the horses come forward nickering in the gloom. The Hungarian stands with head erect, ears pricked forward so that I will recognize he is an animal of importance. The Arab puts his front feet on the lower bars of his corral and poses like a circus performer to show how glad he is to see me. Both are individuals and in their reactions to me, I become an individual. I forget about being cold, and am filled with happiness.

From the beginning of time, relationships between man and horse have been personal. Today we have lost that relationship. In an urban world of computers, life has become impersonal. The crowd swirls around us, yet we do not look at the people we pass in the street. The man who drives to work has no contact with other drivers. The man on the plane does not speak to the passenger who occupies the adjoining seat. We do not wish to become involved; we lose the ability to communicate and we live in a schizoid world. Many of us feel the sense of loss and seek to regain our identity with the land and with the world of nature. In competitive trail riding, we discover that a horse is not only a means of locomotion, he is a creature that opens a whole new world.

2. Sound in Wind and Limb

OBVIOUSLY, it would be a waste of time for a competitive rider to buy a show-gaited Saddlebred or a nervous, fine-boned Thoroughbred just off the track. It would also be a waste of time to look at a horse that was too highly priced. Before getting in touch with a seller, a buyer should decide on the amount he can afford to pay. This makes it easier for the buyer and is a courtesy to the seller, who will not be deceived into thinking he can sell a three-thousand-dollar animal to a person who can afford to spend only five hundred.

Equally important, the buyer should realize that he will not find the perfect horse and that faults will have to be balanced against good points.

With that in mind, he should look for soundness, heart, and compatibility, with the second rated nearly as high as the first, and the third included although many authorities do not mention it.

Under soundness are listed age and conformation, which should not be judged as for a horse show. In competitive riding, performance counts more than comeliness.

The type of horse he chooses will in large part reflect him as a person. (I use the pronoun collectively for both sexes). Usually inarticulate, the horseman will find his reasons for choosing one horse rather than another difficult to explain and he will resent psychological interpretations, for he prides himself on being a simple, uncomplicated individual. If he sees himself as a cowboy in a big hat, is that to be scoffed at any more than the scientist who sees himself in a white coat?

As he learns to know his horse, so will he learn to know himself; therefore it behooves him to select an animal with whom he can be congenial.

From the start, he should beware of the hazards he will encounter. If he has raised the horse, he will consider himself an expert, forgetting that he is as blind to his horse's faults as a mother is to her child's. If he plans to use a horse he has bought, he should remember that Old Pal might do for a jaunt in the park, or for working cattle, but not for the Virginia Ride.

"Pal? Why a hundred miles would be nothing to him. . . . Is that really a bog spavin? And a ringbone, too? Funny, I never noticed — "

If a friend has loaned him a mount, he should forget the adage about never looking a gift horse in the mouth; open wide and make a thorough inspection.

"The vet says he's eighteen instead of eight? Well, now, I didn't know that!"

If he buys a horse, he should remind himself that there is no easier mark than the amateur who enters the horse market. Even professionals are duped from time to time although few will admit it. A man will confess that his new car is mechanically deficient, or that his wife isn't the woman he expected her to be, but never will he confess that the horse he bought isn't exactly what he wanted. This is partly due to ego and partly because the purchaser hopes to resell the horse.

Or if the seller tries to be honest, he might meet with a reaction such as I encountered. A prospective buyer would do well to keep the experience in mind for a variety of reasons.

Looking for the ideal horse (which was my first mistake), I attended an auction, having heard a Thoroughbred mare was to be sold. As a precaution, I called the rancher who had pastured the mare — who, I was sure, would give me an honest opinion.

"Yes, indeed," the man said over the telephone, "the mare would be gentle enough for children. She belonged to a teen-age girl."

Small auctions do not resemble the Keeneland Sale in Kentucky, where Thoroughbreds are sold for thousands of dollars to an audience in evening clothes — and this was a small auction. I sat in the rear of the closely packed tier of seats, and every time the gate opened, my heart beat faster, as I expected to see the mare ridden by one of the girls who reined the horses around the sawdust-floored ring with practiced skill. When the mare finally appeared, she was led, not ridden. Her chestnut coat gleamed, and she held her head high. Her conformation was faultless, and she was not excited by the crowd. In my imagination, I could visualize myself galloping across country on this beautiful creature.

Only one other person bid against me, so I bought the mare for a moderate price. When I had trucked her home, I showed her to my family.

"She's a little nervous," I explained, as the mare pulled away from my hand. "She's in a new place."

I didn't ride her that day, since it was late, but early the following morning I saddled her. Usually I would have lunged a new horse, or asked someone to ride with me, but I was so anxious to try Jewel (that was the mare's name) that I neglected the safety measures a person should take when he has purchased a new horse. I swung into the saddle. The mare would not move, so I increased the pressure of my legs. The next thing I knew, I thudded against a fence post; the world spun around; I couldn't get my breath. The mare stood and looked at me, showing no reaction, not even breathing hard.

The following day, accompanied by my daughter Tex, I rode the mare again, despite increasing pain in my back and one leg. Jewel kept switching her tail and her gait felt as though she were walking on rubber. After many years, horsemen acquire a sixth sense. I turned around and rode back to the stable.

By the horsemen's grapevine, I learned the mare had been stabled at the fairgrounds when her owner had first purchased her, so I went to see the caretaker.

"The mare threw a fellow the morning of the sale," the caretaker said. "The man who told you she was gentle for kids was standing there watching. That mare's a bad actor; the girl never could ride her."

My ad in the paper read, "Spirited mare, not for children. For sale cheap."

After I had eliminated three youngsters under ten, and the mothers of numerous girls who indignantly assured me that their daughters could ride any horse alive, I settled on an older, experienced horseman. He was a nice fellow, and I told him the mare had thrown me.

The man smiled. "That'll happen every now and then."

To the man, I was a timid woman who knew little about horses and less about bargaining, but I was glad to get rid of Jewel, even if I took a loss.

When the pain did not go away, I went to a doctor with the result that I spent the next ten days in traction in a hospital, and for nearly a year I could not ride, but I was more fortunate than the man to whom I sold Jewel. The first time he rode the mare, she went over backward, and when the man was lying half conscious on the ground, she tried to kill him by striking at him with her front feet.

After that, I lost track of Jewel, but she continued to haunt me. What had made her the way she was? Finally I located the man who had raised her, and drove to his ranch to see him. His name was Buster, and I was sure he was rough with his foals.

"Yeah, I remember that mare — by my Thoroughbred stud outa a mare called Fancy. Couldn't never race Fancy; she was too mean, so I used her for a brood mare. Jewel was her filly, just like her. First time I saddled her she threw herself on the ground and screamed. I figgered she musta been cinch bound."

To this day I wonder if the mare tried to get rid of her rider because the cinch hurt her, or if she was born, as some people are, with psychopathic tendencies. Whatever the case, I hope that the mare was not bred, or if she was, that I will never unsuspectingly buy one of her foals.

If this is an example of how not to buy a horse, what then is the proper procedure?

If possible, a veterinarian or experienced rider should accompany the novice purchaser, although even the novice should know the points of a horse, and be interested in learning about unsoundness and blemishes. If a horse goes lame in the show ring or on the track, a veterinarian or trainer will care for him, but if he goes lame on the trail, miles from a checkpoint, his rider has to diagnose and treat the problem.

Let us suppose that a buyer has made an appointment with a horse breeder who has been recommended as honest, and that he is accompanied by a knowledgeable friend who has ridden in Competitive Rides. The coffee has been drunk in the office (in the West, it's in the kitchen); the trophies have been displayed by the breeder, who is acting as though he really does not want to sell a horse, but is glad to conduct a sight-seeing tour, while the visitors evince more interest in the goats than the bay gelding that the breeder just happened to have brought in from the pasture that morning. It might, however, behoove the visitors to observe the stallions and the mares. How do they react to the visitors? Are they gentle and curious, or are they nervous and frightened? What is the disposition of the stallion who sired the horse that is for sale? Are the stallion and mares good examples of their breeds or crossbreeds? Are the paddocks and stalls clean?

In this case, appearances speak louder than words. The man who treats his horses well is apt to be more honest than the man who is rough and neglectful. Also, the well-fed, well-cared-for horse will usually prove to be sounder and easier to handle than the horse that has not received good care. Horses are like children — abuse, a ghetto environment, illness, and injuries uncared for will present problems in later life.

Eventually the breeder gets around to the bay gelding, who is haltered and led out of the stall, and here again the visitors should employ their powers of observation. Is the wood of the stall chewed? If so, the horse could be a cribber. Do the sides show signs of being kicked? While the horse was in his stall, did he wave or sway from side to side?

Stable vices are difficult to cure, since they are signs (as they are in humans under comparable conditions) of a deep-seated neurosis.

The breeder, holding the lead rope, says, "You can see this horse has good bone."

The friend immediately becomes pokerfaced and mutters a noncommittal "Mmmmmm," while the buyer wisely decides to remain silent.

The friend knows that "bone" refers to the circumference of the legs below the knees and the size of the hocks, as compared with the weight they must carry over distances — an important consideration in competitive horses.

"Can we see him outside?" the friend asks.

The buyer follows the horse and two men through the barn door. He likes the bay gelding, but it is hardly the dashing, high-headed beauty of his dreams.

The friend is more practical. He is getting a general impression of the horse, examining him in profile from the front and the rear, observing that the bay, like many horses, has some good points and some not so good. What is important is that he has no serious fault that would disqualify him.

The horse is of a size suitable for the buyer, a little over fifteen hands, which is average. A large horse is not necessarily a better weight carrier than a small one. Many large horses are awkward, like large people. Indeed, in years past, it was difficult to sell a large horse for use in the mountains, not only because he was apt to be less footsure than a smaller horse, but also because he was hard to pack and mount on a narrow trail.

What about the proportions? The hindquarters are equally developed with the forelegs. If one were developed at the expense of the other, it would mean either a strain on the forelegs due to propulsion from muscular hindquarters, or strain on the hindquarters because of overmuscular forelegs.

A fault, but not too serious, is the fact that the bay is not as "well ribbed up" as he might be; that is, his barrel should be rounder behind the girth, the body deeper, the ribs longer to generate lung power.

The friend hunches his shoulders in his coat, his breath frosting the air. For some reason, it is usually cold when one buys horses, but the prices

SOME POINTS OF THE HORSE

1. Poll
2. Withers
3. Girth
4. Loins
5. Croup
6. Shoulder
7. Elbow
8. Forearm
9. Knee
10. Cannon
11. Pastern
12. Coronet
13. Fetlock
14. Stifle
15. Gaskin
16. Hock

are apt to be lower than they are in the spring, and the horses are fuzzy-coated. If they tend to be fractious, they will show it when they are ridden. As real estate should be seen in the drabness of winter, and prospective spouses under stress, so should horses be seen off season. Then shiny coats will not cover a multitude of sins.

Now for the parts of the horse one at a time, starting with the head, which should be not too long or coarse, and in harmony with the rest of the body. The forehead should be wide, the nostrils large, and the eyes well placed. Much can be told about a horse's disposition from his head. Can't we tell a great deal about a person from his face? A Roman nose on a horse, besides being unsightly, can signify stubbornness and a tendency to be heavy in hand, while a bump between the eyes should be regarded with suspicion. Captain Horace Hayes, Fellow of the Royal College of Veterinary Surgeons, called it, in his time, "the fatal bump", and declared an animal that he portrayed as an example to be "a rascal of the deepest dye."

Do the ears perk forward to sounds and moving objects? If they do not, the animal may be stolid in nature or ill or even drugged.

The ears should be small and alert although that can be a matter of preference. Some breeders prefer lop ears, which they say are a sign of a placid disposition.

Are the eyes intelligent? Not all animals have large, liquid orbs like those in the Victorian portrait of Pharaoh's Three Horses; but small, close-set eyes (as in humans) are another sign of a "rascal of the deepest dye" and who would want a horse that fits that description?

Hollows above the eyes usually denote age, similar to bags beneath the eyes of senior citizens.

The bay is standing slack-hipped, his head down, his ears aslant in the worst possible pose. Horses customarily do this when their owners want to show them off. The breeder could curse. Instead he moves the bay forward to show him at better advantage.

"How old is he?" the friend asks.

"Seven," the breeder replies, knowing that this is a rhetorical question, and that the friend will accept his word for the moment. Later he will look in the horse's mouth.

Next the neck, which should correspond with the length of the fore-legs, not with the dimensions of the body, and should be well set. Thoroughbreds tend to have long necks which steamline them for speed; that

SKELETON OF THE HORSE

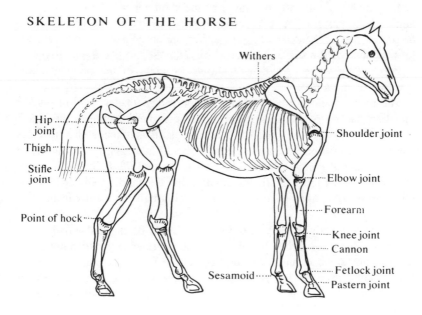

is, the long neck muscle draws the forelimb forward to a greater stride. A short, thick neck denotes pulling power, which is desirable in a cart horse. For the competitive animal, a happy medium is desirable. Too long a neck makes a horse rein like an eel, and tends to overweigh the forehand by bringing forward the center of gravity. Too short a neck makes a horse rein like a tank, and puts undue strain on the front legs.

A ewe neck is a definite fault for a competitive horse, for he does not see where he is going and he is difficult to handle on rough ground. The term is used to describe a neck that is thin and concave instead of being arched.

The withers, which are the summit of the spine between the neck and the back, should be fairly high for leverage and should extend to the rear to permit a good neck carriage and free movement of the shoulders. Since many of the muscles and ligaments that control the forehand are attached to the withers, their importance cannot be overemphasized. If the withers are too high, they will be rubbed sore by the saddle; if too low, it will be difficult to keep the saddle in place. Attention should also be directed to muscular development along the withers. If too skimpy, there will be weakness; if too thick, shoulder action will be hampered.

The shoulders should be long and sloping at approximately a 45- to 55-degree angle. Frequently the angle of the shoulder will be similar to the angle of the pastern. A short, straight shoulder means the horse will be heavy on the forehand and he will suffer undue concussion on the forelegs, which could result in what cowboys call "a gait like a pile driver."

Look at the elbows, too; they should be clear of the body to allow freedom of motion.

The back should not be too short or too long. (Later we will discuss the short-backed Arab.) Too short a back can mean a choppy gait and a tendency to overreach. Too long a back decreases the ability to carry weight. A roach back (that is, a convex back) is unsightly and interferes with the way of going, while a sway back is a definite fault, for it means the weight is borne by the ligaments and that the saddle will cause sores. Old horses sometimes have sway backs, although the fault can be congenital.

The area directly in back of the saddle should be flat and broad.

The hindquarters: From the rear, if a line is drawn from the point of the hip straight to the ground, it should bisect the hock, the cannon, and the hoof. Hips that are too high show weakness. The loins and thighs should be well muscled. The stifle, like the elbow, should not be too closely bound to the body.

PROPER CONFORMATION

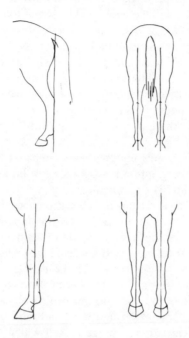

At this point, our buyer is becoming confused. He's growing cold, but he doesn't like to mention it. The friend ignores him, and so does the breeder, both of whom are engrossed in the fascinating game of one-up-manship.

All the points studied by the friend thus far are important, but none more than the legs, which are for carrying weight, for support, for flexion and for extension. The legs aid in distributing concussion, a paramount consideration of competitive rides which demand trotting over hard, rocky ground uphill and down steep grades.

The forearm should be wide and thick, the muscles long, not bunchy. The cannon should be flat and shorter than the forearm. The bone and tendons below the knee should be smaller in comparison to the knee; otherwise the horse would have what in people is termed "piano legs." However, if the cannon and tendons below the knee are too slight (a common fault), the horse will be what is called "tied in below the knee," a definite weakness for a competitive horse. The fetlock should be thick and wide in proportion and free from blemishes; the pastern should be of medium length and shape to take concussion. If it is too sloping, the flexor tendons will pull and the heel break down; if too straight, there will be excessive concussion on the leg and a predisposition to ringbone, navicular disease, and other unsoundnesses.

The hocks should be wide, deep, and of similar size. The feet too should be the same size, although the forefeet, which are for pulling and weight carrying, are rounder than the hind feet, which are for pushing and for power. The angle of the hind feet is a little steeper than that of the forefeet. Another thing to note is the wall of the hoof, which should not be thin or brittle.

The buyer beats his hands together and stamps on the ground to keep his body from congealing into a block of ice. With any luck, the friend should be through with his examination.

But in this the novice is mistaken. He has only seen the preliminaries.

The novice stamps his feet again, his breath smoking on the chill air. The leafless branches of the trees form webs against the grey sky. The frozen pastures and the fuzzy-coated horses in the paddocks are beginning to dampen the novice's enthusiasm. He is inclined to agree with Boswell, the famous chronicler and biographer of the eighteenth century, that "for my own part, I think. . . . to get astride a horse's back, and be jolted through mire, perhaps through wind and rain, is a punishment too severe for all the offenses I can charge myself with."

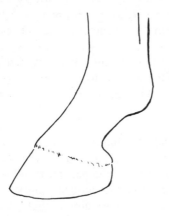
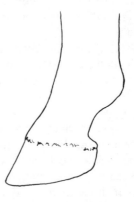

Normal pastern   Too short pastern

THE TEETH

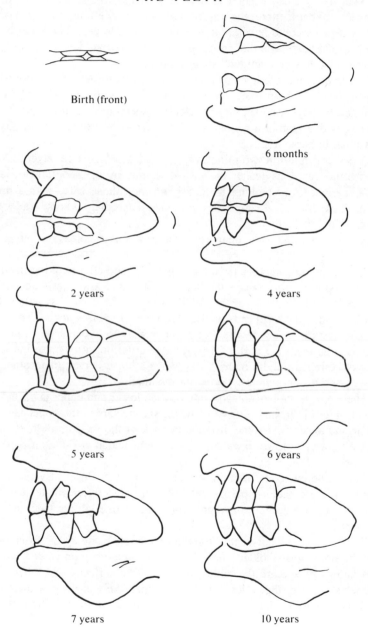

Birth (front)

6 months

2 years

4 years

5 years

6 years

7 years

10 years

What had seemed a good idea in August has lost some of its attractiveness. What is more, the novice wishes he had left his friend at home, for by now he could have come to a decision. He probably could have, but it would have been the wrong one. While no one likes to be cold and ignored, the novice's attitude betrays the amateur.

The knowledgeable horseman is never impatient; he is meticulous and thorough. If he hasn't been born with these traits, he has learned them.

When he buys a horse, he is not only inspecting an animal, he is also dealing with a man or a woman — and never underestimate the ability of a woman in horse trading.

A dealer can tell in two minutes how much a prospective buyer knows. To the unscrupulous dealer, the easiest victims are the people who, lacking experience, are looking for a bargain, and those who, with a minimum of experience, imagine they are experts and that no horse trader can make a fool of them.

A little learning is a dangerous thing when it comes to buying a horse.

The friend now approaches the bay gelding, and after stroking his neck and speaking to him, grasps the horse's upper and lower jaws and opens the mouth to look at the teeth. While a horse of a good disposition will not fight this, much depends on the skill with which it is done. The teeth are the best indicators of age, but accurate only to five years. From five to nine, the teeth are still a fairly reliable criterion; after nine, the teeth cannot be relied on. In many areas, when a horse is more than nine, the description of the animal is "smooth-mouthed."

There are six molars on each side of each lower and upper jaw, making twenty-four in all, and in front of them, six incisors in the upper jaw and six in the lower. At some distance in back of the incisors on both sides of the upper and lower jaws are canine teeth, which are seldom apparent in mares.

Like children, colts have milk teeth, which they lose. By three, the center incisors become permanent. At four, the intermediate teeth are lost and the second ones have grown in; and at five, all the teeth are permanent.

The younger the horse, the straighter the angle made by the front teeth. As the horse grows older, the angle becomes more pronounced. Other indications of age are the tables — that is, the surfaces that meet when the jaws are shut, the yellowing of the enamel, the withering of the gums, and the change in shape of the teeth from square to oval. The teeth appear longer, so that we frequently hear an older person described as being "a little long in the tooth."

The condition of the enamel, type of feed, and vices, such as cribbing, can affect the teeth, making it difficult to verify age, and unless a person is going to buy and sell large numbers of horses or establish a stud farm, it is not necessary to become an expert on judging a horse's age by his teeth. A quick glance at the mouth will tell a knowledgeable person if the horse if five or under, or if he is over nine. If a buyer wants to be certain, he can consult a veterinarian. Don't hesitate to do this, for wise indeed is the person who recognizes his limitations. Only the immature and those who lack confidence claim to know everything.

As Dr. D. P. Hatfield said, "You can't fake it in Trail Riding." This applies to riders, as well as to horses. No beginner can, by studying illustrations or reading reports, become an expert at estimating a horse's age. That takes years of experience. Besides, there are other things for the novice to learn.

In the case of a competitive horses, the buyer should avoid purchasing a colt or filly, as well as a twenty-year-old, for the majority of Rides do not allow entries under five years of age. At the same time, a buyer should not turn down a nine-year-old or even a twelve-year-old on age alone, for many older horses who are in good condition and have not suffered crippling injuries can outdo a five-year old. A sure sign of the amateur is his insistence on a three-year-old, unbroken colt.

The friend, who seems impervious to the cold, now says, "May I see him trot?"

The dealer says, "Sure," and calling, "Come on!" to the gelding, pulls on the halter rope to make the animal trot down the road by the stable, while the friend watches the horse from the rear. The novice, deciding he might as well restrain his impatience, is not sure what the friend is looking for, but he watches too, and because he is afraid of betraying his ignorance, says nothing, which is a wise course in any circumstance.

At this point it is well to remember that the friend is concentrating on the physical aspects of the horse. The observations he is making with regard to the mental qualities will be considered later.

When the horse is being led away at the trot, the friend is concentrating on the hind quarters and the hocks. When the dealer leads the horse toward the stable, the friend looks at the head and fore limbs.

Why is this?

If a horse is lame, the head and neck will jerk up when the injured leg hits the ground. If the horse is lame in both legs, he will travel stiffly. If he is lame behind, one hip (viewed from the rear) will be carried higher than the other.

Major F. C. Marshall, U. S. Cavalry, author of *Elements of Hippology,* wrote that lameness in the rear, which is not easily diagnosed, should be called to the attention of a veterinarian; that it is hard enough to interpret the reason for lameness in the front legs, but that lameness in the rear demands a skilled practitioner. Usually, Major Marshall said, obscure lameness in the rear is in the hock; in the front, it is apt to be in the foot or the ligaments and tendons.

If the friend were to tell the novice how many causes of lameness there are in horses, how many defects there are to watch for, and how many old injuries, the novice might be tempted to make his excuses to the dealer and never darken the doors of a stable again.

This list would not include diseases.

Even to an expert it is a depressing situation, and yet a horse is only as good as his legs. Xenophon, the famous Greek general, declared more than 2000 years ago that no matter how perfect a horse was, if his legs were bad, he was useless for war. The same can be said for competitive riding. A lame mare can be used for breeding, and a horse that is only lame under certain conditions can be ridden as a hack, but to trot forty to a hundred miles over rough terrain, a horse must be "sound in wind and limb."

Therefore, the inspection of the legs must be painstaking and thorough.

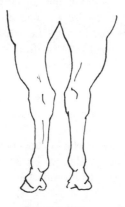

Cow-hocked

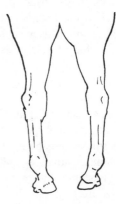

Bowlegged

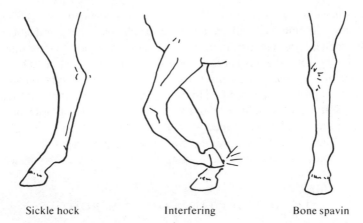

| Sickle hock | Interfering | Bone spavin |

"Look first at the foot," Xenophon said. This the friend keeps in mind. His inspection includes the feet, for contracted heels, thrush, corns, seedy toe, and cracks; but he feels that these problems caused by feet and by shoeing merit detailed explanation. When the novice has bought his horse and started to train for his ride, he will have to learn a great deal about the subject. For the moment, let him rest secure in his ignorance.

As the horse trots up the road, the friend looks to see if he interferes; that is, if he strikes the fetlock with the opposite foot. This can injure the fetlock and is caused by poor action and improper shoeing. Sometimes a horse will interfere if he is tired.

The friend also checks for forging, that is, striking the under side of the shoe or the sole of the front foot with the toe of the hind hoof or shoe on the same side. When this happens, the horse makes a click-clicking sound when he moves. Improper shoeing is the main reason for forging.

If the horse paddles (if he throws his feet out to either side), he should not be considered for competitive riding. The same applies to interfering severe enough that the horse cuts himself, although some people argue that mild cases of paddling or interfering can be corrected by shoeing.

The bay gelding has neither defect, which the friend notes, remembering a Thoroughbred he nearly bought — handsome and intelligent — who paddled. The horse tired quickly, and eventually his knees gave way.

When the dealer returns the horse to the stable, the friend says, "Will you back him, please?"

This maneuver is accomplished easily. If the horse had moved his hind legs with difficulty, or half squatted, he might have been arthritic, had back problems, or had a stifle or spavin. The horse also stands squarely on his front feet, which is another good sign. If the horse places one foot in front of the other, or points a foot, or places his weight on toes or heels, he is probably unsound. However, the friend does not confuse the natural shifting of weight behind for unsoundness. A favorite pose of horses is to stand slack-hipped — that is, with the front feet planted squarely, but one hip assuming the weight while the other relaxes.

The friend now examines the gelding's legs, a step that the dealer has

CROSS SECTION OF THE FOOT

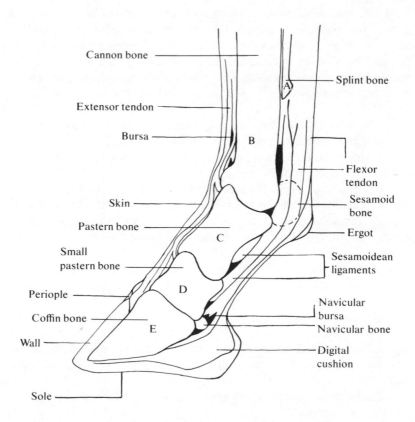

been expecting. If the friend omits one step, he will lose status, for horse trading is as stylized as Japanese art or treaty-making between nations.

With his fingers, the friend feels for fever or throbbing in the coronets and pasterns, which might indicate laminitis or founder. In laminitis, the laminae, which are soft tissues of the foot, become congested with blood. Usually the front feet are affected, although the others may be too, at different times. In chronic cases (that is, when a horse has continued attacks), the hoof becomes misshapen and scaly, and ridges appear on the wall. An X-ray will reveal an alteration in the position of the coffin bone due to pressure. In chronic cases, when the front feet are affected, the horse will draw his hind feet beneath him and extend his forefeet to take the weight off of them. In acute cases, the blood fluids sometimes pressure the outer face of the coffin bone so that it is forced through the sole of the foot. The horse suffers great pain; his temperature rises, and he breathes rapidly.

Causes of laminitis are overfeeding (the pony who gorges on clover or gets into the oat bin), drinking cold water when heated, riding too hard on rocky ground, and overexertion when tired.

Needless to say, a horse with laminitis would never do for competitive riding.

Navicular disease, another affliction horses suffer, is not easy to detect in its primary stages. One sign is for the horse to extend one foot and rest it on the toe. Located in the forefeet, the disease affects the navicular bone, a small bone lying between the lower pastern bone and the coffin bone. The navicular bone is subject to pressure at every stride, and must remain smooth for the tendons to slide over. Should the pressure of the tendons become too great, the bone may become inflamed or break, which, in addition to the damage to the bone, causes the tendons to chafe — a painful injury for any horse.

Navicular disease is incurable, but veterinarians can remove the sensory nerve in an operation called a neurectomy, which enables a horse to perform without pain for a number of years.

Our friend recalls a horse, twelve years old, who was "nerved," and who carried his rider more than 600 miles on competitive trail rides. Buying a horse that has been nerved, however, is definitely not recommended. One disadvantage is that the horse, experiencing no feeling, could suffer a trauma to the foot that would cripple him so badly he would have to be destroyed.

The causes of navicular disease are similar to those of many of the diseases that afflict a horse's feet — riding too hard on a rough surface, faulty shoeing, and sometimes hereditary factors.

The friend now feels the pasterns for ringbone, which results from inflammation in bone-producing tissues. Horses with upright pasterns are particularly susceptible to ringbones, which are caused by overwork on hard surfaces and by sprains. When the ringbones are high on the upper pastern bone, they are not apt to prove bothersome, but if they develop under the extensor tendon or near the navicular joint, they can cause incurable lameness.

Some ringbones are so small as to be hardly noticeable, while others are large, bony protuberances above the hoof.

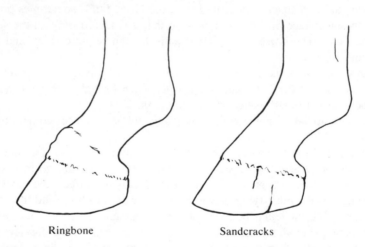

Ringbone   Sandcracks

In sidebones, bony growth results from inflammation of the lateral cartilages, which receive and distribute concussion. These growths appear on the feet just above the coronary band and may not be troublesome in some cases; but if a horse is worked hard on a concrete or rocky road, he can easily become lame from sidebones.

Splints, one of the most common examples of unsoundness, are bony growths on the splint bone and are seen most often on the inside of the front leg. Splints may cause lameness in early stages or at any time, if in a position to interfere with the knee joint or the tendons. Those located well forward or low on the bone are not as serious, and when the inflammation of the injury subsides it seldom results in lameness. Splints are usually caused by concussion or kicks.

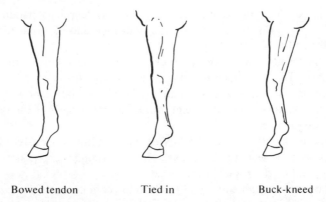

Bowed tendon   Tied in   Buck-kneed

Strained tendons are more serious, in particular a "bowed" tendon that can cause permanent lameness. This is a rupture of the tendon, usually midway between the knee and fetlock, and it is called a "bowed" tendon because of an enlargement in the area that has been injured. Strained tendons are commonly seen in racehorses and horses that have been worked too hard while young. Faulty shoeing, concussion, heredity, and conformation also play a part.

A horse that has had serious tendon problems is a bad risk for Competitive Riding.

Spavins — bone, blood, and bog — are diseases of the hock and are caused by a strain such as overexertion in jumping, rearing, or pulling, excessive concussion, bad shoeing, and, it is suspected, heredity. In bone spavins a bone or bones become inflamed and in time an ossification results in enlargements in the area. Blood spavin affects the vein that runs across the front of the hock, while bog spavin, due to enlargement of the joint capsule, shows in front of the hock toward the inside. As with most horses' leg problems, if they are given prompt attention, they can in most cases be cured or minimized; neglect compounds the problem and may lead to crippling an animal that might otherwise have led a useful life.

A test for spavin, which the friend now performs, is to pick up one back leg, flex it, and hold it in that position for a second or two, then drop it and say to the dealer, "Trot him, please."

The dealer obliges, with a grin, appreciating the friend's routine, which has been established for centuries.

The novice, shrunken into his jacket, wonders if his toes are frostbitten. However, he watches what his friend is doing, not realizing that, in addition to learning about horses, he is learning patience and awareness — traits necessary to good horsemen and of value to men in all walks of life.

As the friend bends over to look at the horse's knees, the novice brightens. This is something that even he can understand. Scars or swelling on the knees would mean the horse had fallen or sustained a blow, and the damage could mean problems, particularly if joints or tendons were involved.

As the friend steps back, the novice looks at him anxiously. Has the horse passed the tests for lameness? But the friend's expression reveals nothing, and he does not speak.

One or two tests remain, in addition to the common ones for lameness. One of these is for blindness. The friend checks for clear eyes, then passes his hand with an upward motion to see if the animal reacts. It is well to remember that the eyes of the horse were adapted for an animal whose defense was flight. Thus the location of the eyes, which enable the animal to see objects at various distances by raising or lowering his head. So far, experts agree that horses cannot distinguish color, although there is some argument in that respect.

Even the novice would not buy a horse with faulty eyesight, although on one Ride a girl entered a horse with only one eye. When the judges queried her at the check-in, the girl said, "I've been riding him for years. He trusts me, and I trust him. We never have any trouble." And they didn't.

At last the friend thinks the examination is over.

Again he is mistaken.

"Shall I saddle him?" the dealer asks.

"Will you, please," the friend says.

The dealer looks at the novice. "Do you want to ride him?"

Immediately the novice is threatened by stage fright. Perform in front of these two experts! He'd forget which side of the horse to get on! Besides, the gelding might be too much to handle.

He steps back. "Why don't you ride him?" he tells the friend. "Then I can get on him later."

The dealer understands the novice's reluctance; so does the friend. Better to recognize one's limitations than mount the horse and, like Lincoln Steffens' famous rider, gallop wildly off in every direction. In a literal rather than symbolic sense, he would not only fail to know what he was looking for, but would confuse the horse as well.

"All right," the friend says. "You can see him under the saddle."

This isn't a bad idea, either.

Most horsemen take their own saddle to try on a new horse; they are accustomed to it, and can concentrate on the horse and not be distracted by a forward-seat Steubben when they are accustomed to a stock saddle. In this case, the friend advised the novice to buy a horse first, and then his equipment.

The dealer saddles the gelding, and the friend mounts, walking down the road; then, as he approaches an open field, he trots — a slow trot, and after that an extended trot, or rather a fast trot, for the gelding has not been trained for the extended trot. Where the ground lifts to a hill, the friend alternately trots and walks. A crow rises, wings flapping, from a grove of leafless willows. Does the gelding shy? A steep bank drops to a ditch, tangled with dried weeds and gleaming with patches of ice. The gelding does not hesitate. He picks his way cautiously, but confidently. If he had lunged or been excited and lost his footing, points would have been counted against him.

When the friend dismounts in front of the stable, he checks the gelding's pulse and respiration — the former by feeling the artery that curves around the jawbone; the latter by counting the movements of the flank when the horse breathes. The friend does not take time to explain to the novice the normal pulse and respiration rates. That will come later in training; but it is important to make sure the gelding has a normal pulse and respiration and quick recovery. If they were abnormal, they would prove a severe handicap for trail riding.

The dealer, unsaddling the horse and replacing the bridle with a halter, says, "If you'd like, you can take him and ride him a few days."

This is a generous offer that is not often made to a prospective buyer; and yet, if a dealer has a good, sound animal, it is a shrewd move. The dealer sees that the novice still envisions a handsome show animal. If the friend keeps the horse in his stable and teaches the novice to ride the gelding, he can explain an all-important point.

"Never select a competitive horse for looks alone. He is not a professional model, he is an athlete."

The novice should, if he takes the horse home, have time to ride and reflect on the gelding; he will not be subject to impulse buying, an all too common failing in the equestrian world.

Of course, the dealer has to be sure, as he is in this instance, that the horse will be well cared for.

Both friend and novice accept the dealer's offer. Price is mentioned; there is no haggling when the dealer is reputable.

3. Horses, Like People, Develop Neuroses

CONFORMATION and soundness can be judged by an experienced horseman or veterinarian, but disposition is not easily defined. Breeders tell us that the offspring inherit conformation, soundness, and disposition from the dam and sire, and that disposition is the most important characteristic.

This is particularly true for competitive riding. No matter how sound a horse is, how well-proportioned and well-bred, if he lacks courage and stability, he will do better as a hack than a competitive horse.

"It's not the size of a horse that matters," a Scots trainer told me; "it's how big his heart is."

Our knowledgeable friend who inspected the bay gelding with the novice was aware of this, and he looked at the dam and at the stallion who had sired the gelding, and while he was checking the gelding for conformation and soundness, he noted what he could of the gelding's disposition.

To understand horses, we must remember that the horse evolved as an herbivorous animal who grazed in herds and whose defense was primarily in flight. He moved over vast areas, feeding as he went. When pursued, he galloped for miles, and, if necessary, leaped obstacles in his path. It was safer to move in herds than alone, so he developed into a gregarious animal, which explains why some horses become depressed when they are isolated; others are not obviously affected although horses are happier if they are with their kind.

In common with other vertebrates, horses share a dominance hierarchy based on recognition of the individuals within their group. In times past, when horses roamed wild, the stallions exercised their authority over bands of mares, fighting any stallions who ventured to challenge their authority. Today, in the pastures, we can see a mare who, by nips and kicks, establishes herself as the matriarch; or a gelding might set himself up as the guardian of a mare and foal. Always there are aggressive individuals who dominate.

A competitive rider should keep in mind that he must recognize a horse's failings as well as his virtues, for horses, like humans, are not without vices. Nor should a person judge a horse by human standards; he should realize that many of the horse's characteristics have evolved for reasons of survival.

For example, horses will frequently drive off a crippled animal if he is put among them in a pasture. They do not appear to want a sick or injured member, possibly because in the past such an animal was a handicap if predators attacked the herd and they had to flee.

Again, Moyra Williams who wrote *Practical Horse Psychology* says that horses show no feeling when another horse dies, no matter how closely associated they might have been. From personal experience, I can say that the remaining member of a team will not work as well in harness with a strange partner but not because he is grieving; his routine is upset. Even in humans, long periods of grieving are not normal; in horses it would seriously impair their efficency and their ability to get along in their environment.

"A horse," wrote James Fillis, one of the world's best known equestrians, "is incapable of affection for man. He (the horse) possesses only habit, which he often acquires far too easily."

This might seem an arbitrary statement and could easily antagonize horse lovers but it might be a good idea to see what Fillis meant.

To illustrate his point, Fillis related the story of a friend who had a horse that greeted him with every sign of affection when he entered the stable. The friend felt the horse was genuinely fond of him and would suffer if he were to leave. Fillis asked the friend to lend him the horse for a few days. After learning the friend's routine, he rode and fed the horse exactly as the friend had done, even imitating the friend's voice and the carrot tidbits. In forty-eight hours, Fillis resumed his normal voice but continued the riding and feeding routine, whereupon the horse showed the same affection for Fillis he had shown for the friend. Apparently he did not miss his former master in the least.

From personal experience, I know that if I feed Mazda the first thing in the morning, he greets me with nickers but if I pass the paddock without feeding him, he ignores me after the second day, particularly if he is with another horse; and if daughter Tex feeds him, he nickers at her as he did to me previously.

Before criticizing Fillis, it should be remembered that he said that it was to horses' advantage not to be affectionate for if they were capable of affection *as we define it in man,* horses would obey only one master and would suffer neuroses and breakdowns when sold. Their lack of this human trait has survival value.

It does not in any way contradict the affection of horses for their owners who have treated them kindly and are riding them at the moment. A horse performs best for one person; he knows what to expect and he trusts his owner. He develops in every respect while the livery stable hack becomes indifferent and often has vices. He is ridden by so many people that he becomes confused and torn by conflicts.

To a certain extent, the behavior of all animals is influenced by experience which shows some degree of learning. In horses, the process is largely the response of the organism and its environment; that is to say, the adaptation of the animal's behavior of the moment to the problem he encounters in his environment.

What do we mean when we speak of a horse's disposition? Horses are remarkably varied, but fundamentally consistent, as are humans. The sensitive, nervous animal will remain so during his lifetime, while the stolid animal will remain stolid. A horse's disposition might be defined by the sameness of his reaction throughout his life to the stimuli in his environment.

However we define it, we must recognize that horses are not unfeeling, characterless animals that can be treated alike. Horses are individuals, as are men, and must be handled accordingly. The competitive rider must never forget this. Experienced riders sometimes experiment with four or five horses before they find one that suits them, not for reasons of soundness, but of disposition.

While disposition, as we said, is difficult to define from a horse's appearance, it can be identified to some extent. In all breeds, the head is expressive — the eyes, the ears, the nostrils, and the lips. Vindictiveness and stubbornness can be glimpsed in little pig eyes; kindness and intelligence in large, liquid orbs. Or curiosity or fright or suffering. Horses that have white scleras can be confusing, since frightened or angry horses roll their eyes, revealing the whites, while some horses naturally have white scleras but are not mean. An example was my mare, Voodoo, seven-eighths Thoroughbred, but an Appaloosa with the Appaloosa eyes, as well as markings. When Voodoo turned her head to look at me, she showed her feelings as clearly as a person. Why was I late with her grain? Didn't I realize she shouldn't be kept waiting?

I also had a Thoroughbred racehorse at one time with a "wall" eye, and when he rolled that eye at me, I knew he was up to deviltry.

The eyes of ponies, half hidden by forelocks, are particularly expressive: "I will not budge a step further, and no one can make me," or, "What shall I do to get into mischief?"

My Arab, Mazda, has large, almond-shaped eyes, and if I confine him alone in the small corral, he hangs his head over the rails, gazing at me so reproachfully that I can't bear to look at him.

The ears act in conjunction with the eyes; forward and quick-moving to show curiosity, alertness, apprehension; back against the head to display anger; slack from boredom.

If a horse is frightened, his nostrils dilate and he snorts. If he is about to kick or bite, he draws his lips from his teeth. At the same time, his ears flatten and his eyes shine with anger. Some horses will also lengthen the upper lip to show displeasure or stubbornness.

"Ordinarily," wrote Armand Gaubaux and Gustav Barrier, the French veterinarians, "the faculty of expression of the head is in direct relation with the purity of the race."

Undoubtedly breeding plays an important part in a horse's disposition. When horses have been bred for centuries for certain characteristics, those characteristics become dominant. An example is speed in the Thoroughbred, and combined with it, a sensitive, higher-than-average intelligence. Or would it be more exact to say a higher-than-average sensitivity to environment?

Many Arab and Thoroughbred breeders, past and present, believe that blood horses, if not spoiled in the breaking, have more courage than cold-blooded horses.

The blood horse is easily identified. He has quality, is slender, tall if he is a Thoroughbred, not so tall if an Arab; he has the well-formed head characteristic of his breed, good withers, long muscles, good but fine bone, and small feet; on his thin skin the veins show easily — if an Arab, the skin is black; when in good condition, he is responsive, alert, and full of vitality. Some horses of this type can be too nervous, too excitable. Thoroughbreds that have been raced frequently fall into the category. They seldom relax, are delicate eaters; if ridden, fight to be in the front, plunge and pull on long rides, tire themselves by fretting.

Such a horse is not for competitive riding. Voodoo was inclined to be that way, although she fretted inwardly rather than outwardly, so that no matter how well-conditioned she had been, she sometimes arrived at the noon lunch stop so tired that the veterinarians debated holding her over. And yet it never occurred to her to give up. She would have gone until she dropped. Amazingly enough, she drew on inner reserves, so that by the time she crossed the finish line, she recovered sufficiently to place well in the lightweight division.

The cold-blooded horse, like the blood horse, should be considered in relation to his environment.

These cold-blooded horses are stouter built than the blood horses, with heavier bone, usually a rougher coat, larger feet, and heavy growths of hair on the fetlocks and around the mouth. They do not react as intensely as the blood horses to outside stimuli, and tend to be more stubborn and lethargic, but they can also be remarkably obedient and reliable. In a crisis, they are less apt to panic than a blood horse, and on occasion can show more wisdom than their riders, when it comes to estimating the perils of a swamp or boulder-strewn stream.

Men who lead pack strings into the wilderness areas (when they don't have mules) prefer cold-blooded horses, insisting that they are more sure-footed and level-headed than a blood horse, especially a Thorough-bred. During the hunting season, they pack bear carcasses on the backs of the older animals. From personal experience, I agree with the pack-ers. It is a nightmare to ride a fretting Thoroughbred who does not watch where he is going over a mountain trail, whereas it is a pleasure to ride a wise animal who knows where to put his feet and does not shy when a deer leaps from the forest.

The fact that a pack string travels at a rate of two and a half to three miles an hour should not be a criticism of the cold-blooded horse. He was not bred for speed.

On the other hand, it would be incorrect to say that by training and conditioning, some blood horses cannot make good trail horses. Indeed, the Arab is one of the outstanding competitive horses. As in most cases, it is a mistake to generalize.

Courage — what horsemen call heart — may be found in both the blood horse and the unregistered animal. We see it in the Thoroughbred who wins the Grand National or the 900-pound Arab who comes in first on the 100-Mile Tevis. Or the fleabitten grey a boy rode to round up a herd of mares that had escaped from the paddock. So ancient and de-crepit was the grey, that the boy's parents felt he must be put down, al-though the boy begged to save his friend. The grey cut off the mares with the skill of the cowpony he'd once been, his sides heaving and streaming sweat; he didn't stop until the mares were back in the paddock where the boy slid from his back and wept with his head against the trembling flanks, knowing he'd won a reprieve for the gallant old fellow, who had proved he could still do his job.

In nearly every recorded instance of courage and intelligence shown by horses, we find trust between men and animals. Trust derives from mutual respect. Often ignored, the relationship between horse and rider is the vital factor in success, and cannot be overemphasized in competitive riding. A horse should be selected with the same feeling for companionship as a friend — always remembering the limitations of the horse. If you expect a great deal from your horse, he should be able to expect the same from you.

Neil ffrench Blake, in *The World of Show Jumping,* quoted an observer after witnessing a spectacular performance by a small British horse, "I think you say to your horses that to prove your love for them, you will show them that they can beat the world. And then you take them out and do it."

Before selecting a horse, it is advisable to do a little self-psychoanalysis. What kind of person am I? Quick-tempered? Do I ride to release tension? Frustration? Am I competitive? Shy? Do I enjoy being alone? Am I patient? Meticulous? Authoritative? Physically timid? Reckless?

The person who is intuitive in his relationships with people will be so with horses, while the person who approaches horses as though they are machines is callous, and should concentrate on automobiles.

Too often the complaint is heard, "I don't like that horse." Why?

The answer is vague. "He won't walk fast enough," or, "He's stubborn," or, "He's spooky."

The reasons are superficial; the real causes for discord are more complex, and have their roots in the disposition of the horse and of the rider. Some people and some horses are simply not congenial.

This was the case with a Palomino I once owned — a strong, well-built animal with a silver mane and tail. To all appearances, he should have been able to carry a rider all day, but he was stubborn and unresponsive, and when he was tired, he stopped. Eventually persuaded to move, he trotted in reluctant jerks.

Voodoo, for all her temperament and physical handicaps, made a better competitive horse than the Palomino. Indeed, the Palomino did not qualify at all.

Yet the Palomino might have done better if there had been cooperation between us. I did not like the horse, and he did not like me. When he was stubborn, I grew annoyed, which made the Palomino reluctant to do what I wanted him to do. I expected too much of him. I demanded skills that were beyond him, and he reacted in the only way he knew how.

When I sold him to a farmer who rode him for fencing and irrigating, the Palomino was happy, because his owner did not ask him to do more than he was capable of doing.

Mutual trust gives the horse confidence. If his rider believes he can do 100 miles, he will attempt it. The horse is similar to the child who looks to an adult for reassurance and instruction. A horse may be born with a bold disposition, but if he is found fault with, he will soon become nervous and indifferent. Conversely, a timid, highly strung horse may gain confidence from a rider.

Horses are remarkably sensitive to the people on their backs. A horse that will behave beautifully with a confident, knowledgeable person will shy and try to run if he is ridden by a heavy-handed amateur. Or he will turn into a plodder.

Yet the same horse, should a child get on him, is apt to behave like an old plug. Why is this? The child is usually fearless, he does not weigh much, and he is not strong enough to pull on the horse's mouth. Some people insist that the horse is aware of his responsibility and acts accordingly.

Most trainers will agree that horses know whether a man or a woman is in the saddle. Some horses will not allow a man to get on them, or are nervous the entire time a man is riding them. I had a Quarter Horse that my brother rode one day to drag a doubletree at the end of a rope. The horse became frightened, bucked until the rope entangled his legs, and fell. After that, he bucked if a man got in the saddle. The horse was acting not from instinct, but from the association of a man's voice, weight, and way of moving with the unpleasant experience of the rope. A woman, on the other hand, moved differently, spoke differently, and weighed less. No women had abused the horse, and so he behaved well when a woman rode him.

Horses will test a rider new to them, if not the first time they are ridden, usually within a few weeks. These adventures can be unexpected, and sometimes disconcerting. When I rode Mazda before I bought him, he was so slow that I nearly crossed him off my list. Suddenly, one morning after I'd bought him and brought him home and was riding alone, Mazda shied and plunged for no reason at all, and continued to misbehave the two hours we were out. Then he became docile, but if I had not been firm with him, he would have continued to shy and plunge every time I rode him. Like a naughty child, a horse will see how far he can go without being disciplined. If he is not made to behave, he will become more unruly every time his owner rides him.

If a prospective buyer is timid, he should settle for an older, docile animal, for a horse will sense his unsureness and take advantage of it, resulting in nasty incidents that will make riding a trial instead of a pleasure.

The timid rider is easy to identify. He holds tightly onto the reins and sits forward in the saddle, his heels and legs clutching the horse's sides. His tension is relayed to the mount, so that the animal becomes tense, too. An old English print, depicting the cautious rider, described him as having "reached the age of discretion" — something everyone does, and should not be ashamed of admitting. Such a rider can still enter competitive trail rides.

Younger people, too, are frequently timid, although it is more difficult for them to admit their fear.

Some professionals attribute the sensitivity of the horse to the rider as a sign of intelligence. While intelligent horses respond quicker than stupid animals, this does not imply the process of reasoning. Rather, it is a reaction to the rider's legs, hands, and voice.

Intelligence is not as easy to gauge as we might imagine. Not only can a horse's reaction to stimuli be mistaken for intelligence, but play can also fall into that category.

For instance, Mazda will untie his halter and open gates, which might suggest a high degree of intelligence, which it does to an extent; but according to animal psychologists, Mazda was probably bored or felt playful, and started pulling on his halter or the gate for something to do. Discovering that he could free himself and wander about happily, he repeats the performance at every opportunity.

Play is manifested by foals who pick up sticks and toss them about like dogs, or who frolic in the spring meadows. The more alert a foal is, the more apt he will be to play.

On Okinawa we had a horse of uncertain breeding named Brandy, who was one of the American animals shipped from the States to replace the native horses lost in World War II. Anxious to graze on the grass outside the paddock, Brandy lay down on his side and rolled under the fence. This is the sort of story that people enjoy telling about their horses, but such stories do not demonstrate the skills in which the horse excels, and are as unjust a test of a horse's intelligence as tapping out numbers or nodding the head in reply to questions. These are tests that should be reserved for man and the higher vertebrates.

As with humans, horses develop neuroses, and again, like humans, some horses are more susceptible than others. While they do not inherit the neuroses, they may be born with a genetic weakness that predisposes them to breakdown. A horse that might go all to pieces under one circumstance might not be affected by another that would panic his stablemate.

Of equal importance is how an animal is raised. If he is well-fed, handled firmly but kindly, and allowed the freedom of a pasture, he will not be so apt to develop vices, although this cannot be predicted with certainty, since other factors must be considered, one of which is conditioning—not the term as we use it in getting a horse in shape for competitive trail riding, but the term that can best be explained as an unconscious form of learning which Pavlov, the Russian physiologist, called "conditioned reflex." This is best illustrated by the dog that began to salivate when he heard the bell ringing that announced the arrival of food. I also think of a rickety truck that is used to distribute feed on a stud farm. When the horses hear the rattle of the truck, they run to the feed boxes or begin to pace up and down the fence in their eagerness to get their grain.

These reflexes are unconscious and form the basis of many fears, likes, and dislikes in animals. The most conscientious breeder or trainer may not be aware of conditioning in his horses.

Conditioning depends on continued association; that is, the horses had to hear the noise of the truck many times before they began to associate it with their feed. Unlike conditioning, imprinting need not be due to a continued series of events. During the early weeks of an animal's life, and at certain other times, the animal is unusually susceptible to what Konrad Lorenz calls 'object fixation.' Lorenz studied object fixation in greyleg geese, but another example is a calf my brother bottle-raised, and that followed him around for weeks, thinking my brother was its mother. Little study has been done on imprinting in horses; however, it might be said that imprinting plays a part in the development of the foal who is turned out in the hills with the herd and the foal who is kept in a stable. The foal in the first instance learns from the older horses how to take care of himself, while the foal in the second instance is dependent in later life.

The competitive rider who does not know the background of the horse he buys is at a disadvantage. The veterinarian might certify that the horse is sound, and the buyer might be satisfied with his conformation, but how is he to know that the horse was nearly drowned when he was a colt, and so becomes panicky when he sees water? Or that because of rough handling or idleness he has developed certain vices?

The more sensitive and intelligent a horse, the easier he is to spoil. He can take to rearing, or bucking, or bolting, or shying.

The kind of rearing to be concerned about is not just standing on the hind legs, as some horses do when they feel good, but rearing to get rid of the rider, which is dangerous, since the horse can go over backward. Nor does bolting mean galloping over the fields when an animal is full of grain and wants to run; it means bolting blindly, the eyes bloodshot, regardless of obstacles. I had such a horse, which ran me into a tree. These horses run with their chins down against their chests, or their heads in the air, and are nearly impossible to stop, although if a rider is in a field, he can shorten a rein to guide the horse in a circle. The best method to avoid a runaway is to sense when the horse might take off and shorten the reins, talking all the while.

An even better policy is not to have such an animal, for bolting and rearing are vices almost impossible to cure, and hazardous for a trail rider.

Shying is not so dangerous, although a rider may be unseated if the horse whirls. Shying can be induced by playfulness, by the rider's timidity, or by defective eyesight, or some previous experience of the horse. Some horses give only a little start; some plunge and whirl. The horse should never be whipped or forced up to the object that frightened him. The rider should talk to him, either remaining in the saddle or getting off and leading him toward the spook he imagined in the bushes, or the orange-colored bulldozer. On a Trail Ride, a horse will encounter all sorts of new and strange sights.

Horses who kick usually do so because children or dogs have teased them, or because they are frightened, and striking out with a hind leg is a form of self-defense. Even the gentlest horse might kick, so it is wise to watch out for a horse's heels when near him. A thwack on the rump can be dealt to the offender, but it must be administered immediately. At distance events, kickers are identified by a red or orange ribbon tied to the upper part of the tail, and are avoided by both contestants and judges.

Bucking is another vice and one that is all too common, although there is a difference between the horse who feels good, giving a few jumps when he starts on a Ride, and the horse who tries to throw his rider on the trail. Some bad-tempered or spoiled horses can always be depended on to buck. If a horse "feels his oats," it is advisable to lunge him before mounting, and once in the saddle, to hold up his head. If he can't get his head between his legs, he can't buck. A few miles on the trail at a trot usually settles a horse.

Biting is also a vice that is particularly irritating on Trail Rides, where large numbers of horses are congregated and people are moving among them. No one likes to be bitten by a horse, particularly judges who mark down horse and rider for manners. Biting customarily results from feeding horses sugar or teasing them, and can best be dealt with by a smack on the nose accompanied by a vocal reprimand.

Whatever the case, punishment should never be meted out in anger. The rider who loses his temper only frightens the horse into panic or hostility.

". . . gentleness, great patience and no violence," Fillis wrote. Also firmness and prompt punishment.

Idleness and boredom play important parts in many vices, as they do with people. Add to this the treatment that results from ignorance, greed, and cruelty, and it is no wonder there are so many spoiled horses.

The wise horseman, if he has a difficult animal, will try to discover why the horse acquired the vice. This is done with humans, so why not with animals? If the cause of a vice is known, it will be easier to cure. I learned this lesson with Voodoo, who hated box stalls and kicked whenever she was confined in one, or when she was in a trailer, which created problems in transporting her to Trail Rides and at Rides that demanded horses be kept in box stalls. Indeed, at one Competitive Ride, she became so upset that she developed colic and had to be given a shot by the veterinarian, which eliminated her from competition, since no Ride allows drugs or medication. Not until I opened the stall door, leaving only a halter rope across it, did she calm down. Then she munched her hay peacefully in the moonlight, while I worried she might have colic again. I sat up all night watching her, shivering in a blanket.

Wretched beast.

Not until some time later did I learn from Voodoo's former owner that when she's been in training as a racehorse, she'd been heavily grained, blanketed, and confined in a closed box stall until she'd become uncontrollable. A human would develop claustrophobia under such circumstances — why not a horse?

I was never able to make Voodoo like closed places, but by feeding her grain in an open-door stall that allowed her to come and go as she pleased, and by using a halter rope or stall guard to confine her in a box instead of shutting the door, I was able to ride with her in competition.

If I hadn't understood why Voodoo misbehaved when she was confined, I might have thought she was being ornery and punished her, and then she would have been worse than ever, and I would not have been able to use her on Trail Rides. Indeed, one might say that ignorance on the part of the owner is a major contributor to vices in horses.

4. Which Is More Important, the Individual Horse or the Breed?

DISTANCE RIDERS should know the characteristics of the various breeds and crossbreeds that make them suitable for the trail, and how these horses have performed in the past.

But first it might be a good idea to define breed, a term that is used indiscriminately and often incorrectly.

"A breed," explain Dr. William Jones and Ralph Bogart in *Genetics of the Horse,* "is a group of animals that breed true in regard to a certain set of traits. If these traits are more than one or two in number, then the inbreeding necessary to bring them into the homozygous condition will also bring other less desirable traits into the homozygous condition. This entire package of traits will then give the horse its breed characteristics. The more inbreeding that is practiced over the years, the more distinctive the breed will become."

The charts of the Tevis (Endurance) and the Bitterroot (Competitive) Rides for the last ten years show nearly every type of saddle horse known in the northern hemisphere, including Morgans, Appaloosas, Quarter Horses, Arabs, Thoroughbreds, Standardbreds, Mustangs, crossbreeds and grade horses. The records of the Eastern Competitive Trail Ride Association, the North American Trail Ride Conference, and the American Endurance Ride Conference show the same thing. In the first official Endurance Ride held in this country in Vermont in 1913, and in subsequent military trials, Arabs and Morgans predominated. There were also a fair number of Thoroughbreds, a few Irish Hunters, Anglo-Arabs, Kentucky Saddle Horses, and Standardbreds.

The earliest Rides in the United States were sponsored at different times by the Morgan Horse Club, the Arabian Horse Club, Army Remount, U.S. Department of Agriculture, and various individuals interested in seeing if one breed or combination of breeds was superior to another in performance. Rivalry was keen among the horsemen concerned.

In any discussion of breeds, the Arab should be considered first, not only because his is the oldest registry, but because of the infusion of Arab blood in most of the other breeds.

According to many authorities, the true Arab was the horse of the Bedouin nations of the Nedj, a high, desert area east of Medina, and of the tribes of the Syrian desert. Water was scarce and there was no pasture on which to graze. To survive, the Arab developed great powers of endurance. He could carry weight and exist on sparse rations. He lived close to his owner's tent and he ate figs and fruit, as well as barley and chopped straw.

To me it is interesting that when I am lunching on the trail, Mazda will steal my orange if I am not looking.

A characteristic of the Arab is a high tail carriage, a broad, bulging forehead and concave profile. The eyes are large, the neck arched at the crest, the chest is powerful, the bone is slender but dense; the back is well-muscled and short. Arabs are supposed to have one less vertebra than other breeds, and many of them do, but pure-blooded Arabs have been known to have the usual number of vertebrae, while some horses of other breeds also lack a vertebra. The croup, W. R. Brown, author of *The Horse of the Desert,* says, is slightly higher than the withers, which I heard an endurance rider say was a disadvantage in going downhill. Brown said it contributes to speed, since the hindquarters propel and a low forehand throws weight in front.

Capt. Horace Hayes, Fellow of the Royal College of Veterinary Surgeons, wrote that the best Arabs do not exceed 14.1 or 14.2 hands. However, some pureblooded strains are taller.

The performance records of the Arabs, historically and today, are impressive. Lady Ann Blunt, founder of the Crabbet Stud in England, wrote that, "the Arabians seem capable of going on for surprising distances, under heavy weights, without tiring."

In 1971 the President's Cup winner of the North American Trail Ride Conference was Kandar, a twelve-year-old purebred Arab gelding, weighing 850 pounds and standing 14.3. The horse participated in 21 Rides during the year, was ridden 1000 miles in competition and traveled over 20,000 miles by trailer.

In 1970, 1971, 1972, 1973, and 1975, the Tevis Cup Ride was won by an Arabian, Witezarif, ridden by the experienced endurance rider, Donna Fitzgerald.

A rider who is buying a horse might be inclined to favor the Arab when he learns of their performance records, but he should not be too hasty. Another type of horse might suit him better.

What about the Thoroughbred?

The Thoroughbred is best known to the public who, when Thoroughbred is mentioned, pictures the winner of the Kentucky Derby or a hunter taking a jump at Madison Square Garden. Not many people identify the Thoroughbred in competitive trail riding, and yet the Thoroughbred has actively participated in many Rides.

As most people know, Thoroughbreds trace their pedigrees in the male line from three Arabian stallions imported to England in the late seventeenth and early eighteenth centuries. These stallions passed on to their descendants the conformation and disposition of what became, through judicious breeding, the Thoroughbred who excelled in the increasingly popular sport of racing. Before 1775, horses were raced as four-year-olds over long distances, carrying big weights, but after 1786, the emphasis was on running two-year-olds and early maturity of the foals. Endurance was sacrificed for speed. On the track today we are apt to see Thoroughbreds that are fine-boned and highly strung. Hunters and steeplechasers are more apt to resemble the old-type Thoroughbred, which is more suitable for distance riding.

Incidentally, the term "hot-blooded" applied to the Thoroughbred has basis in scientific fact. The Thoroughbred has a higher blood volume and a higher amount of hemoglobin than other saddle horses — appreciably higher than the draft animal.

Anyone who has owned a Thoroughbred knows what a pleasure they are to ride. I had a mare sired by Flying Scott, too slow for the track but with the lovely fast walk, the long trot and free-swinging gallop characteristic of her breed. Unfortunately she was sickle-hocked and too light-boned for a competitive horse. This lack of bone is the biggest handicap to Thoroughbreds in competitive riding.

The Thoroughbred stands from 15.2 to 17 hands, has long, sloping shoulders which give him his stride, prominent withers, flat bone, a fine head, small feet and silky skin. Traditionally the Thoroughbred has great courage which, with his intelligence, are his most admirable traits.

That the Thoroughbred can win and place in endurance and competitive rides has been proven more than once. In 1922, Capt. Herbert

Watkins of the 13th Cavalry rode a Thoroughbred gelding, Norfolk Star, to win the 300-Mile Endurance Ride at Colorado Springs, Colorado. Norfolk Star was seven years old, stood 16 hands and had a short back and well-sprung ribs. The weight carried was 200 pounds. The 60 miles a day was covered in nine hours minimum, eleven hours maximum. Speed counted 40 points and condition 60. The trail was a different one each day, but the return at night was to Colorado Springs.

At the final judging on the day after the finish, Captain Watkins said that Norfolk Star felt so good that the Captain could hardly make him stand still to be judged. He completed the 300 miles in 47 hours, 37 minutes.

The same year a Thoroughbred won the 300-Mile Ride at Fort Ethan Allen, Vermont. In 1924, a Thoroughbred took fourth place in the 300-Mile Ride at Warrenton, Virginia, while Thoroughbreds have consistently placed and won in the Virginia 100-Mile in Three Days Ride at Hot Springs.

Thoroughbreds are more commonly seen in eastern Rides than in western events. I do not recollect one registered Thoroughbred entered in the Bitterroot Ride, while North American Trail Ride records show few of the breed. As an experiment, Richard Barsaleau, D.V.M., trained and rode a Thoroughbred mare in the 1973 Tevis. The mare was five years old, stood 16 hands, weighed a little over a thousand pounds and had good bone. She finished the 100 miles in approximately 18 hours, showing excellent recovery the next day. Again, in 1974, the same mare finished ninth out of more than 125 horses, completing the Ride in 14 hours. If a rider prefers a Thoroughbred, Dr. Barsaleau said, he sees no reason not to ride on Endurance trials. But it should be remembered that Dr. Barsaleau, in addition to being a veterinarian judge, is one of the most experienced competitors in the country.

From this it can be seen that the Thoroughbreds have their proponents, as well as the Arabs.

Equally devoted to their breed are those who raise and ride Morgans, and it might be said with good cause, for the Morgans have also excelled in competitive riding. They were entered in the first official Ride in 1913, sponsored by the Morgan Horse Club. Since then a 100-Mile Ride held annually at Woodstock, Vermont, long a center of Morgan breeding, has carried on the tradition.

Due to the efforts of Walt Disney, most Americans know that the Morgan breed was established by Justin Morgan, but what people do not realize is how exceptional it is for a breed to be established by one stallion. He stood only 14 hands and weighed 950 pounds. In contests staged by his owner, he usually managed to out-pull and out-trot — under harness or saddle — whatever rival was set against him. Seldom has so much willingness and heart and amiability been seen in a little horse.

Morgans stand from 15 hands to 15.2. Today there are two types—the old-fashioned Justin Morgan animal that is stocky, with a short back, rather heavy neck, small ears, and well-muscled chest and legs. The second type was bred before the registry was closed by the introduction of Standardbred blood to promote longer necks and legs, more prominent withers, and greater height.

The Morgan has been popular for years in the West, as well as in the Northeast, for he is well suited to the mountains. His small size enables him to negotiate narrow trails. He has stamina and he is sensible and willing.

In the first U.S. Endurance Ride, held in 1913 in Vermont, a Morgan placed second, and again a Morgan placed second in the 300-Mile Military Trial at Fort Ethan Allen, Vermont, in 1922. In 1955 a registered Morgan won the Florida 100-Mile in Three Days Competitive Ride.

A recent registry is that of the Quarter Horse, who is also popular in all parts of the country for competitive riding, although he is best known for racing and for working with cattle.

The Quarter Horse first appeared in the American colonies, a mixture of Spanish blood from the south and the southeastern equivalent of a Mustang. These horses were crossed with imported English animals, mainly Thoroughbreds. From this breeding evolved a thick-set little horse that was able to get off to a quick start and run at an amazingly fast pace for a quarter of a mile. Hence the name Quarter Horse. As more Thoroughbreds were introduced into the eastern United States, interest declined in the smaller animals and they were used mainly by settlers moving to the southwest.

As is the case with the Morgans, there are two types of quarter horses—one is the 14-hand average animal with a broad chest, short back, hugely muscled legs, short stout cannons, and a short head with alert ears. Anyone who has seen this type in a cutting exhibition knows they have cow sense and that they can move with the speed and agility of a circus performer. In addition, they are amiable and smart, but they are not as suitable for trail riding as the other kind of Quarter Horse: the racing animal so closely resembling a Thoroughbred in some instances that it is difficult to tell them apart; and indeed the infusion of Thoroughbred blood has been heavy. These horses are not as tall as a Thoroughbred, although they have much the same conformation.

The 1966 Bitterroot Competitive Trail Ride was won by a 16-hand registered Quarter Horse, while another Quarter Horse placed high in 1974 in the Tar Heel Ride in North Carolina, as well as numbers of other eastern and midwestern Rides.

Horses that are not as familiar as the others, but that have excellent records in the Rides in which they have participated, are the Hungarians. The original Hungarian was a small, tough horse, a descendant of the horses ridden into the plains of eastern Europe by invaders from the Asiatic steppes. In the early part of the 19th century, the Hungarian government established stud farms and began systematic importing of the best Thoroughbred and Arab blood available. The result is the modern Hungarian that is of three types — the Shagya, or Arab; the Nonius, a medium-to-heavy ride and drive animal, standing 15.3 or over and also under 15.3; and the Furioso, who is lighter and stands from 15.3 to 16.2.

Horace Hayes, in *Points of the Horse,* said, "These horses have sound legs, good hocks, plenty of bone, intelligent heads . . . particularly enduring, stand both hot and cold weather well . . ."

I might add that they have a long, swinging stride that is a delight to ride, are alert and sensitive, and have great courage.

Hungarians were frequently ridden over long distances under difficult circumstances in the wars that beset Europe from ancient to modern times. In 1892 an official Endurance Ride was held between the Austro-Hungarian army and the German military. The route was Berlin-Vienna and the winner was Count Starhemberg, riding a Hungarian mare, who covered the approximately 350 miles in 71 hours, 27 minutes.

In 1963 a Hungarian gelding, a grey, standing approximately 16 hands, won the Florida three-day 100-Mile Ride. In 1971 Hungarians won the lightweight and heavyweight divisions at the Virginia 100-Mile in Three Days Ride at Hot Springs. A year or so later, a Hungarian gelding won the New Jersey 100-Mile in Three Days Ride. A Hungarian also placed in the Top Ten in the Tevis.

One of the most popular horses on Competitive Rides is the Appaloosa. People are apt to think of the Appaloosa, or Appaloose, as the cowboys called him (shortened to Appy today), as a distinctly American horse. This is not so. Spotted horses were depicted in early Oriental art and in medieval European illustrations. Ponies have been seen in Mongolia with Appaloosa marking, and in Denmark there has long been a registry for spotted horses called Knabstrub.

Nevertheless, it is in the United States that the Appaloosa has attained his greatest prominence, and here he is identified with the Nez Perce Indians who bred the spotted horses in the Palouse County of eastern Washington — unique for the fact that Indians did not, as a rule, indulge in constructive horse breeding.

These horses are 14 hands or over. For permanent registration they must have the Appaloosa coat pattern and breeding stock must have the white sclera, striped hooves, and mottled skin.

In recent years the Appaloosa received infusions of Quarter Horse, Thoroughbred, Saddlebred, and Arab blood. Voodoo, for instance, was 7/8 Thoroughbred and looked like one, except for her smaller size and markings. The average Appaloosa is heavier than Voodoo, with a strong back and well muscled hindquarters and legs. A good example of an Appaloosa would be a top stock horse.

From its Nez Perce pony ancestors the Appaloosa has inherited toughness and good sense.

One of the newest registries is that of the Spanish Mustang. *Mesteno* was the Spanish name for this horse, but the word was too difficult for Americans to pronounce, so they changed it to Mustang. Mustang breeders claim that their horses are descended from the horses, which were mostly Barbs, brought over by the Spanish. These horses, who escaped in Indian raids or were otherwise lost from the Spanish settlements, ran wild on the plains and in isolated mountain valleys, where survival was harsh. In the deserts there was little feed and in the mountains deep snow in winter. After a few generations of existing in the wild state, these horses developed, or, it could be, regressed, into small animals of all colors, with short legs, round barrels, wide chests and short necks. The croup was customarily sloping and the tail set low. What these horses lacked in conformation they made up in alertness, smartness, and unbelievable toughness.

Today there are reserves set aside for wild horses, one of which is in the Pryor Mountains of southeastern Montana; another is in Nevada. Periodically, horses are rounded up and sold so that the range will not become overgrazed.

Proponents of the Mustang are as enthusiastic about these horses in competitive riding as are those who favor other breeds, and like them, can point to performance records.

One of the most interesting stories about a Mustang was told by Colonel Richard Dodge, a well-known frontier soldier and author. The

Mustang, a pony, belonged to a man who carried the mail from El Paso, Texas to Chihauhua, Mexico once a week and back the next. Because of the Apaches, the man had to hide by day and ride by night. The distance between the two settlements was 300 miles, which the mail carrier covered in three consecutive nights. At the end of each trip he rested his pony for four days and then repeated the journey, which he continued to do for six months. The weight carried approximated 200 pounds. As far as Colonel Dodge could see, this remarkable pony suffered no ill effects.

One of the first registered Mustangs I saw was a rangy buckskin stallion, standing about 15.3. He was entered in the Bitterroot Ride and ridden by Emmet Brislawn, whose father, Robert, established the Spanish Mustang Registry.

When Emmet weighed in as a lightweight, Mr. Brislawn darted over. "Put on your chaps, Emmet, so you'll gain more. Heavyweights always win."

Mr. Brislawn had no scientific reason for this belief, but Emmet did as he was told. Robert Brislawn was an old man who had spent more time on the range than in a schoolroom. He had faith in the Spanish Mustang and made it known to the American public. Indeed, every breed owes its existence to such dedicated believers, whether they be the Sultan Nassar of Arab fame or Robert Brislawn.

The Mustang Spanish Fox won the 1965 Bitterroot Ride, and since then Mustangs have been entered in the Tevis and in 100-mile endurance Rides in Nevada.

The Standardbred might be mentioned, too. The Standardbred has more body than the Thoroughbred; is not as tall and not as long-legged. He won his fame as a trotter in races, a gait that is suitable to distance riding, since the trot is the favored gait over the long miles of trail.

Also, there are the Palomino and the Pinto. In all there are more than 35 breed associations and registries in the United States. We have mentioned only those who are most numerous on Competitive Rides.

More popular than any single breed are the crossbreds. That is, the Arab-Thoroughbred or the Anglo-Arab; the Standardbred-Morgan; the Appaloosa–Quarter Horse; the Morab or Arab-Morgan; and the Thoroughbred-grade. A crossbred does not command as high a price as a registered animal, and frequently the rider finds a combination of traits in a crossbred that he cannot find in a purebred. For instance, a Thoroughbred might give speed and heart to a grade mare who might provide stamina. Or a Saddlebred might give size to an Arab. When the United

States had mounted troops, the majority of the horses were crossbreds, mostly with infusions of Thoroughbred or Standardbred.

A remarkable feat of an unregistered horse, attested by official U.S. Army reports, was that of a 7/8 Arabian named Kingfisher on the Campaign into Mexico in 1916. Kingfisher stood 14.3, weighed 925 pounds and was four years old. He carried a weight of 200 pounds and covered 900 miles in forced marches with no hay, over desert and mountain. Forty horses died, but Kingfisher returned with a loss of only fifty pounds in weight. Some years later Kingfisher placed second in the 300-mile Military Trail Ride from Fort Ethan Allen, Vermont to Camp Devens, Massachusetts. The distance was sixty miles a day for five days in not less than ten and not more than twelve hours daily, the horse carrying a weight of 200 pounds. Kingfisher's time was 53 hours, 21 minutes.

A more recent example of an outstanding grade horse was the gelding named Casey, owned and ridden by Bev Tibbits of Morago, California. Casey, ancestry unknown, won the NATRC national championships when he was eleven, twelve, and fourteen years old. At age ten he won the President's Cup, the top NATRC award; and at age fifteen, he placed in the Top Ten at the Tevis.

From this it can be seen that too much emphasis should not be placed on breed.

Conclusions drawn by the riders and judges on the military endurance trials in regard to the type of horse best suited for competition are enlightening, and are as pertinent today as they were when they were written, despite what has been learned since then about stress in long distance riding.

Mr. W. R. Brown, who sponsored a number of the Rides, wrote: "It was found that in addition to sturdy conformation, represented by deep chest and great lung capacity, a short back, powerful forearms and quarters, good bone and sound feet, ability to travel straight on all four legs without interference was a prime requisite, and that the slightest interference ultimately disqualified the contestant."

Captain Herbert Watkins, who won the Colorado Ride in 1923, added, "The horse must have courage and the firmly expressed desire to go ahead. . . ."

Mr. Brown concluded: "Endurance, speed, and soundness are not the exclusive possessions of any one breed of horses and types, but are a combination of many necessary qualities in the individual, combined with training and hard work and a certain amount of chance, which lends zest to any sporting event. . . ."

5. Where Do We Start?

To CONDITION a horse for distance Rides is not easy. The amateur should not imagine that all that is necessary is to throw a saddle on his horse and take off. Or that Old Pal on whom he's been pottering about in the ring is fit to do 35 miles in six and a half to seven hours. Distance riding demands care and conditioning of the horse, and unless the prospective contestant is willing to acquire the knowledge and apply it by hard work, he might as well continue to potter about on Old Pal.

No matter how late it is, whether it is freezing or a hundred and ten in the shade, the stall must be cleaned, the horse fed, groomed, and exercised. Two months of conditioning should be the minimum for Competitive Rides. Three months is a better time, and four if the horse is green. In the case of the Endurance Rides, the conditioning program should start from eight months to a year before the event.

Tex does not enjoy getting up in the morning. Still, when she was training the 3/4 Hungarian, Flower Child, for the Tevis, she set the alarm at six. I do not mind getting up in the morning, but my energy is at a low ebb in the afternoon, and many times I longed to stretch out beneath a tree after a tough training ride on Voodoo. Instead I groomed a sweaty, dirty animal.

The work is menial, but there is a job to be done and incentive for doing it, which contributes to a feeling of happiness and well-being. This, as much as the competition itself, makes the sport worthwhile. Indeed, many an individual who would not touch the grooming brush might envy the mental and physical health of the rider in blue jeans.

The care of the distance horse starts with a proper environment, which might be taken for granted but is ignored by many people. Recently I saw horses standing in mud to their pasterns in a paddock near Monterey, California. In a month I passed the paddock half a dozen times, and each time the horses were standing in mud. In the Southwest I've seen horses in a desert pasture with no shade against the fierce rays of the sun. If I look out the window, I can see half a dozen horses on a nearby hill which is fenced with sagging strands of wire and has been grazed to bare earth. Any horseman can cite similar examples of substandard environment that might be called equine ghettos, and the animals who have to exist in them the underprivileged. When neighbors or the Humane Society object, they are greeted with amazement. What's wrong? The owner's accomodations might not be much better than his horses'; or he might not be much smarter; or he honestly might not know how to keep an animal.

Pastures should never be overgrazed or crowded. There should be clean water and the fence should be of wooden rails or barbless wire, tightly strung. The worst abuses in this respect occur at farms where owners board their horses for the winter. If an owner cannot keep his own horse, he should inspect a number of places, realizing that few people can afford to board a horse cheaply and give it the care it should have. In a crowded pasture a few dominant horses will get most of the hay; if one has influenza, the rest catch it, too; the meek horse will be kicked and bitten. If accomodations are in a barn, the stalls might be dirty, the ventilation poor, and the animal forced to stand day after day in a cold, confined space.

Stalls should be large, well-ventilated, and regularly cleaned. The feed boxes should be of some material that will not break, as should the buckets. Above all, cheap plastic buckets should not be left around for the horse to split into pieces. Straw or wood shavings can be used for bedding. When I am reluctantly wielding the pitchfork, I encourage myself by thinking there is no place that smells as badly or is as sloppy as a dirty stall, and no place as inviting as one deep in fresh straw, with the sun slanting in the open door and the manger full of hay. A clean environment is a requisite for a healthy horse.

Since Voodoo would not go into a box stall except to eat her grain, the maintenance was no problem.

Mazda, on the other hand, will stay in his stall all day if I do not close the door to keep him out.

Voodoo is tied up with complexes; Mazda has none. Flower Child is a different personality from both the mare and the Arab. A cream dun with amber eyes, Flower Child is a vigorous horse who stands 15.3 and weighs 1200 pounds. He is intelligent, level-headed in emergencies, but too strongminded and energetic for an inexperienced rider. He gets bored if he stands around, and he enjoyed his training for the Tevis, which was to be his first Ride. Tex had trained him as a hunter in Fort Sill, Oklahoma, and a rapport existed between them that enabled the two to communicate without speech or aids. I knew Tex was concerned that Flower Child would suffer harm in some way on the Tevis. Whether he made the Top Ten or completed the Ride was not as important to Tex as the well-being of the horse.

Anyone who has had any experience with Endurance Rides has seen horses with colic and thumps, which we will discuss later. Tex and I saw a horse collapse on his feet struggling to get up a hill, while his rider beat him with a stick. The horse died before he reached the crest. Vet checks cannot always guarantee against poor conditioning and ignorant riders, but to do Rides justice, 99 percent of the competitors do know what they are doing and the judges manage to catch the high-risk horses.

The conditioning of Voodoo and Mazda was not as strenuous as that of Flower Child, since they were being entered in Competitive, not Endurance, Rides, but the personality of all three horses played a part in their training, as did their age and weight.

First they were inspected by a veterinarian. An athlete has a physical before he begins training; so should a horse. A blood test shows an animal's overall condition. Is he anemic or does he have a bacterial infection? To function properly, the muscles need an adequate supply of oxygen, which is supplied by the red blood cells. In a poorly conditioned horse, the blood tests differ from those in a healthy horse.

Anemia is frequently caused by parasites or worms. Since it is estimated that the majority of horses have worms, the veterinarian should have a sample of the feces to determine the type of parasitic infestation. As to extent, many veterinarians say this cannot be diagnosed accurately. Whatever the case, the feces will at some time or other show signs of worms. These parasites penetrate the lymph system and the blood, liver, heart and intestines. In addition to anemia, which saps vitality, they can cause colic and sometimes even death. Outward signs are a dull coat and a listless attitude, but I have seen fat, shiny horses that had worms. Worming should be routine. For strongyles (bloodworms) and ascarids (roundworms), use anthelmintics, which are a commercial deworming medicine. For bots, the veterinarian tubes the horse. In our climate, this is after a frost in the autumn. Usually the procedure is repeated in three weeks in order to get the larvae that matured since the first tubing.

The teeth should also be checked. An infected tooth or teeth with rough edges can make a horse reluctant to chew, which means he does not digest the proper amounts of food. The veterinarian can float (file) the teeth. If one is infected he can reduce the inflammation. Wolf teeth, which are the small teeth in front of the first premolar, can be taken out, for they are unnecessary and often irritate the horse when a bit is in his mouth.

In addition, the horse should have shots for tetanus, eastern and western sleeping sickness, influenza, and distemper, and a Coggins test for equine infectious anemia — a test some authorities claim is not infallible. In the West, many owners vaccinate for leptospirosis; a number of states also require VEE shots. Thus, if a person intends to transport his horse some distance, he should ask his veterinarian what shots are needed in addition to those he already has. The vaccination records, incidentally, are not the same as a health certificate. That is separate and is a necessity for trailering horses and for entering many Rides.

Horses that have been in hilly pastures have an advantage over horses that stand in box stalls, for they are exercising in a natural environment, and are mentally as well as physically better adjusted to begin training.

The Hyannis Ranch in Nebraska, where many endurance horses have come from, turns its young horses out to run in the hills. The Bitterroot Stock Farm in Montana does the same with the Hungarians. Probably the majority of western half breds and grade horses have the same background. If horses have not been allowed to run in the hills, the prospective contestant will have to take that into consideration in his training.

Horses are better off to begin training if they have been conditioned within the last eight months; that is, if they have been on Rides the season before or have been hunted or subject to rigorous riding. They will not be as difficult to get into shape as the horse that has seldom been ridden or the horse that was once conditioned but has been allowed to stand around for several years.

Voodoo had been conditioned as a racehorse, but for the last five years she had been in a small pasture and had produced three foals. Mazda had never been conditioned and was much too fat, while Flower Child had been in good shape two years previous, but had been ridden little since then.

Naturally the too-fat horse will have to be worked up gradually to top condition, and his program for training will not be the same as for the horse that is in good shape to start with. Thus it is important for the owner to evaluate his horse before he starts working him for the upcoming Rides.

6. Shoeing Is an Art as Well as a Science

ONE OF the first matters to attend to is shoeing. The horse, unless he lives in the Sahara or a sub-irrigated meadow, cannot be ridden for a long distance without shoes, and this means four shoes, not two "tacked" onto the front feet. The majority of Rides state in entry blanks that all horses must be shod. Unfortunately this does not solve the problem. Judges see numbers of poorly shod horses, including some entered by experienced riders. Inevitably these horses go lame, or if they finish the Ride without being eliminated, develop troubles at a later date.

We have learned a great deal about the care of horses' feet since the Egyptians wove sandals of grass to protect their mounts' hooves. Genghis Khan fitted his war ponies with rawhide cups, and iron shoes were first nailed on in the fifth century B.C. One of the most significant things we have learned is that shoeing is an art, for it takes an expert to tell to a fraction if the hoof is level or how to shape a shoe to a malformed hoof.

Matthew Mackay-Smith, D.V.M., one of the authorities on the equine foot, says that to properly care for horses' feet it is first necessary to understand their functions, which are for protection, support, shock absorption, and circulation.

We can see what Dr. Mackay-Smith means if we look at an illustration of a horse's foot. The bones of the leg are similar to a column that supports the weight of the horse and rider. When the leg comes down at a trot or a gallop, much of the weight is first received by the frog, which, when pressed down, spreads and forces the bars outward. At the same time, the plantar cushion also receives a pressure and spreads, forcing the lateral cartilages outward. The frog and plantar cushion, which are elastic tissue, absorb most of the shock. Weight is also taken by the wall and the bars.

THE FOOT

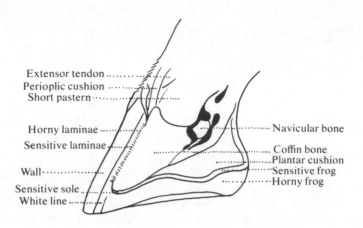

Extensor tendon ....
Perioplic cushion ....
Short pastern ....

Horny laminae ......
Sensitive laminae .....

Wall ....

Sensitive sole ....
White line .....

Navicular bone
Coffin bone
Plantar cushion
Sensitive frog
Horny frog

Now look closely. The column of bone that supports the weight of horse and rider is hung in a sling in the wall and bars by the fit of the sensitive laminae into the horn laminae. As the leg comes down at a trot or a gallop, these laminae, like leaves, yield so that the coffin bone and sole can descend. Additional shock is taken by the flexor tendon moving over the navicular bone. The spreading out of the elastic parts when the foot comes down is termed *expansion*. When the foot goes up and the weight is removed and the parts return to normal, the term used is *contraction*.

As for circulation in the foot, the sensitive structures are filled with capillaries which fill with blood when contraction occurs; during expansion, the blood is forced out.

The foot is indeed one of nature's mechanical miracles, and any interference or injury can be serious, as the experienced trail rider well knows. That is the reason he *never* shoes his horse immediately before a Ride; he does so at least a week or a week and a half ahead of time.

Ordinarily the farrier will appear on a six-week schedule. Since his appointment book is apt to be full, it is well to set a shoeing date ahead of time. Never employ a man who is rough, or the horse will fight every time he uses a rasp. A reliable farrier is low-voiced, patient, and skilled at both hot and cold shoeing.

The owner should know, other than by the fact that six weeks has elapsed, why his horse needs reshoeing. Usually the hoof grows about a quarter of an inch a month, which means a new hoof every ten or twelve months. In a dry, warm climate, the hoof grows faster than in a wet climate, and a healthy young horse's hooves will grow faster than the hooves of an older or sick horse. Also, the hooves of a horse in training will grow at an increased rate.

The owner can check to see if the shoes are worn thin, if the nail clinches are projecting more than normally from the wall, if the shoes are loose, or if the feet have grown too long or wide for correct fit.

Picking up the forefoot, the owner should inspect the hoof wall. Does it look as though it had grown faster at the toe than near the heel? This happens when a shoe has been left on too long, and the reason is that the shoe is nailed fast at the toe, but not at the heel, and every time the weight comes down on the foot, the heels are pressed down against the iron shoe and so suffer wear.

THE SOLE

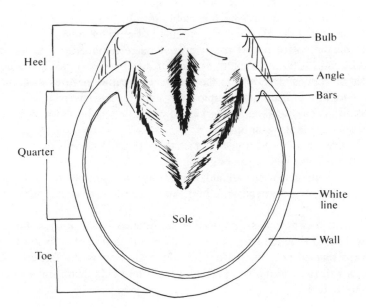

Sometimes the pressure is so great the hoof wall indents or channels out the shoe toward the heels. This growth of the toe gradually draws the shoe forward, making it too short. At the same time, the general growth of the hoof has the identical effect on the shoe as the foot of a teen-age boy who outgrows his boots.

Due to excessive wear on hard ground and to trotting over long distances, the competitive horse may need to be reshod more often than an ordinary saddle animal. This should be watched, for too frequent shoeing can result in nail holes that cause cracking and breaking of the wall. At times, however, a competitior might not have a choice, which is what happened to a lieutenant on one of the military 300-mile Endurance Rides. His horse's shoes wore down so badly during the day that at night, when he returned to the stable, he pulled his horse's shoes, let him rest, and in the morning reshod him for the day's competition.

Some authorities believe in leaving the shoes off for a few days between shoeing; others feel this might encourage cracks and splits. In this argument it might be safe to say that environment and the individual horse play important parts.

Not many people have blacksmith shops today, since most of the farrier's work is done for people who have from one to four horses, but with today's new improved shoes a shop is not as necessary as it once was. Also, many farriers have portable forges.

The morning that the farrier is coming, I tie up the dogs. If it is cold, I put on the coffee pot; if it is warm, I make lemonade. Then I catch Mazda, who is trying to undo the bars of his small paddock, put a heavy halter on him, and tie him to the fence, whereupon he tries to untie the halter rope, a project that occupies him until the farrier arrives.

Mazda is easy to shoe. If he kicked or bit or fought, the farrier would have nothing to do with him.

"I have enough well-trained horses to work on," he tells me. "I can't risk getting hurt by a mean one."

The competitive rider should know this and be able to pick up his horse's feet, walk around with him, and teach him to stand still and not pull back.

Only if a person has the greatest confidence in the farrier should he allow him to shoe the horse alone, and even then it is often better to hold a horse than to tie him, but this should be left up to the farrier. Some horses will rub and nibble at their owner if he holds them, but will stand quietly if tied.

Mazda's feet are clean, and he has been sprayed with fly dope so that he will not fidget. The farrier looks to see how Mazda stands on the level. Then I lead the fat, flea-bitten creature up the road and back. Mazda has not worn one side of the shoe more than the other. He does not interfere or appear to have other problems.

We decide on ordinary, flat shoes in front and small caulks on the heels of the hind shoes, which is how the cavalry horses were shod for the military endurance trials. The shoes are light; I insist on that, for even if the shoes weigh no more than a pound apiece, imagine how much weight the horse raises on a long ride, when his foot lifts from thirty to sixty times a minute.

Mazda is fortunate to have good feet. Corrective shoeing can *help* the horse that interferes, forges, paddles or has stone bruises, corns, cracks, laminitis, or any of the other ills of the feet to which horses are prone; but corrective shoeing is *not a cure* and the owner should recognize that, in some cases, he has an unsound horse. A wise thing to do in this instance is to talk the matter over with both a farrier and a veterinarian. If the opinion is that the horse might go lame if ridden long distances, don't enter him in competition.

Should corrective shoeing be necessary, the owner should not stand over the farrier and tell him what to do unless he is very knowledgeable indeed.

If a horse has stone bruises or if he is going to trot on rocky trails, he can be shod with pads. I put pads on Voodoo when she got stone bruises as a result of having her sole pared too close by an inexpert farrier; my own fault for not watching what the man was doing.

Pads indirectly protect the foot from concussion and can be of various materials, the most common being leather with a packing of oakum soaked in pine tar. The oakum is put in next to the sole; then the leather pad is cut to fit the hoof; after that, the shoe is nailed on. Pads can also be of neolite, neoprene, rubber, or plastic; however, many Rides do not allow pads, so prospective competitors should check the rules. If a Ride allows pads and the going is rough and rocky, pads can be put on and then taken off and the horse reshod for a Ride that prohibits pads, but keep in mind the dangers of too-frequent shoeing. Unless a horse has foot problems, pads are not a full-time necessity.

A comparatively new innovation are Easyboots, which are made of urethane, come in a variety of colors, and can be easily slipped off and on, something like Genghis Khan's rawhide cups. If a horse loses a shoe on the trail, he can be outfitted with an Easyboot, but Easyboots should only be used in emergencies and not for long periods.

"What about borium?" I inquire.

A person can learn a great deal from a farrier and should never hesitate to ask for advice.

"Borium," the farrier says, "will make the shoe last longer and will give the horse traction."

Pure tungsten carbide particles in a mild steel flux (so the farrier explains) are melted onto the shoe, usually in the place of caulks, but some people feel it has a disadvantage—with the resulting improvement in traction a horse cannot slide his foot, which puts undue strain on tendons and pastern bones.

The farrier ties on his leather apron and picks up his tools. After pulling Mazda's shoes, he trims and rasps the hoof walls so that they are level. I hold Mazda, who turns his head to investigate the farrier's hat as he bends over, but I bring Mazda around before he can take the farrier's hat off with his teeth and drop it in the dust.

Leveling the walls is important, for they must balance so that both sides bear the weight equally; sidebones or ringbones can result from one part of the hoof taking more pressure than the other. Strain can be put on tendons and ligaments, too, if the toe is left too long or cut too short. In addition, the heel must be the correct width so that it can contract and expand. In general, the line of the hoof should follow the line of the pastern.

Neither the sole or frog should be excessively cut or pared with a knife. The sole protects the foot from bruising, and if it is pared too closely, the horse will become sore-footed, the sole gradually drawing the walls of the quarters inward, resulting in contracted heels. Another practice common among farriers is to rasp too much of the wall after the shoe has been put on in order to make the foot look better. This is injurious to the horny surface of the hoof. Some farriers are also careless about where they put the nails; if too far down, the wall cracks; if driven into the sensitive part of the foot, the horse goes lame.

The farrier straightens up, wiping his forehead. I tie Mazda to the fence and produce the lemonade. Mazda unties himself and goes over to the creek for a drink. Horsemen who demand obedience from a horse on every occasion disapprove of my permissiveness, but I feel that if a horse is allowed freedom in certain respects, he will develop as an individual. I do not have to be a Prussian to exact obedience when I need it. A horse, as I have remarked, is similar to a child and a child needs to explore.

When the farrier is gone I look at Mazda's feet to see if they are dry, which they are, so I decide that I will make him stand in the damp area by the creek for a while, after which I will put a waxy preparation on the hoof. There are a number of commercial preparations to spray or wipe on horses' feet, some of them with a lanolin base. In the past we used a pine tar and fish oil mixture. Actually it is better for the moisture to come from the hoof itself. The horn, I've been told, is made up of a network of tubules, and the moisture, derived from the blood supply, is contained in these. Good sound feet are mostly a result of proper nutrition and lack of abuse.

If a horse's feet are overly damp and smell, he may have thrush from standing too long in a filthy box stall or wet ground. Thrush, a fungus, is quite common. When it occurs, use a drying agent such as iodine, liquid bleach, or a commercial mix to wipe on the frog and the sole.

Above all, the owner should not forget about the feet just because the horse is shod. He should add their care to his other chores.

7. Some Feed Alfalfa and Some Feed Grass Hay

A VITAL part of conditioning for distance riding is nutrition, for food provides energy and builds and repairs the body. The various kinds of food aid in bone-making, in the production of energy, and in building and maintaining muscles, body tissues, and organs. Building requires proteins (nitrogenous substances). Carbohydrates contribute to energy, while minerals such as salt, lime, and calcium keep bones healthy. Fibrous materials in the food aid in the animal's digestive processes, and water (the horse's body is 80 percent water) aids in blood circulation and muscle operation. Some elements aid in more than one process.

We might look first at the various types of feeds, and then progress to the amounts, keeping in mind that the endurance horse competing in a number of 100-mile Rides is not fed as a novice animal entered in one 35-mile Ride, and that age, the horse as an individual, and environment are important factors.

Not everyone agrees on which diet brings the best results, either for the endurance or the competitive horse. One reason is that quality and type of feeds differ in various parts of the world. On the Oregon coast, I commented to a friend that his pasture was green and lush.

"Yes, it looks good," the friend replied, "but the grass has little food value. It's mostly water."

In other areas, the hay lacks calcium and phosphorus. In addition, alfalfa might be cheaper in some places than timothy, or corn might be cheaper than oats. In the Southwest, pellets, usually combined with some roughage, are a common feed due to the high price of hay, but hay is within reach of most horsemen in the northern Rockies and on the Plains.

On Okinawa, where hay was prohibitive because it had to be shipped from the States, our horses were fed boiled sweet potatoes.

So the availability and price of feed play an important part in the horse's diet. Custom does, too. In the northern Rocky Mountain states, alfalfa is considered cattle feed; timothy is reserved for horses.

"The hay in the Blackfoot Valley," people say, "is better than the hay in the Bitterroot."

Or people boast about bluegrass in Kentucky and about limestone pastures in certain parts of the East. From a practical point of view, the horseman should call the County Extension Agent, who will be able to tell him if certain trace minerals, vitamins, or proteins are lacking in local feed.

Most people buy timothy or alfalfa, or, if they live in California, oat hay. Timothy and alfalfa should be fairly green to retain vitamins, and be leafy, not full of sticks. If left in the field too long, they will not have as much protein as if cut sooner, but it is better to leave them in the field than to cut and bale them when wet, for then they mold. On the other hand, if over-mature, they are apt to be dusty. To be certain about hay, the best course is to ask the farmer to open several bales.

Opinion is divided on the respective merits of alfalfa and timothy. Dr. William Tyznik, chairman of the National Research Council's Committee on Horse Nutrition, said, "Alfalfa in all stages is by far the better hay around today, as far as nutrient value . . ."

The five-times winner of the Tevis Cup, the Arabian Witezarif, was fed alfalfa, while a three-day event rider on the east coast, who conditioned a horse as does an endurance rider, said, "Timothy should not be fed unless the animal is used to it."

On the other hand, a consistent winner in NATRC Competitive Rides wrote me that she omitted alfalfa when she was hauling her horse or competing, because alfalfa causes a slightly higher pulse and respiration rate and increased sweating and urination. In our feeding program, we noted the same disadvantage to alfalfa, and so fed mostly timothy, with an occasional flake of alfalfa, but as it happens, good timothy is available in our part of the country at a reasonable price.

Opinions also differ in regard to supplemental feeding, and this again is influenced by location. In some places there is a shortage of iodine and people feed kelp to offset it, but an overdose can be dangerous and most authorities recommend a block of iodized salt. As we know in the case of humans, iodine is a requisite for the thyroid gland to function properly, so that the body metabolism will be normal. A block of salt should be available to the horse most of the time unless he is a compulsive eater of the mineral, which some horses are; in that case he will have to be fed the necessary amounts by his owner to avoid salt poisoning.

Two of the most important minerals, calcium and phosphorus, are present in hay and grain respectively. As yet, nutritionists have not determined the exact amounts necessary for the horse; indeed, studies are inconclusive in regard to nearly all the trace minerals and vitamins. However, nutritionists agree that a balance should be maintained between calcium and phosphorus which would depend on the amount of the minerals in the hay or pasture. The age and weight of the horse must also be considered. These two minerals are particularly important, for they contribute to the formation and the maintenance of bone. At Cornell University researchers found that lameness is frequently caused by skeletal disorders, which in turn are caused by mineral malnutrition, and that mineral malnutrition can worsen some other injuries. High-phosphorus diets, the researchers said, cut down the efficiency of calcium intake so that if a person feeds his horse too much corn or oats, he runs the risk of creating a calcium deficiency in his horse. Therefore, care must be taken to balance calcium and phosphorus.

Vitamin D, some scientists feel, helps a horse utilize and absorb calcium and phosphorus.

Copper, manganese, zinc, iron, and selenium are all trace minerals. In the eastern United States and many other areas, there is a lack of selenium, while in part of the Rocky Mountain states and in the Dakotas there is an oversupply. According to some authorities, too much can cause what is called alkali disease, which leads to chronic nephritis, while too little might contribute to azoturia. If vitamin E is present in certain amounts and in certain cases, there does not appear to be a necessity for as much selenium, and if selenium is present in certain quantities, there does not seem to be a need for as much vitamin E. However, exactly how the vitamin and mineral are interrelated is as yet not determined.

Many experienced distance riders feed electrolytes, ionized or dissociated salts that dissolve in the body fluids. The electrolytes important to horses are those that contain sodium chloride, potassium, magnesium and calcium — all elements that are found in a horse's feed, but an additional dose is valuable to make sure than an animal that is working hard will not run short of these vital elements, particularly in hot weather, and thus become unduly fatigued and dehydrated. The additional dose also keeps the horse drinking water. Tex gave Flower Child one teaspoonful a day in his grain halfway through training and during the Tevis;

Some Feed Alfalfa . . . 63

the dose can be as large as a tablespoonful and can also be given in the water. However, it is important that a person not give electrolytes without consulting about the dosage with a veterinarian; every horse differs and too large a dosage could result in serious imbalance.

As for vitamins, most nutritionists feel that the horse will synthesize what is needed from his grain, hay, and the commercial supplements on the market. Good quality hay contains A and B vitamins as well as C, and the nutritionists tell us there is little need for additional A or D.

At this point, we should say that when we mention supplements, we mean minerals and vitamins; roughage includes hay, oat and barley straw; concentrates are oats (whole or crushed), barley, bran, and vegetables like raw carrots. Roughage is a necessity in a horse's diet for bulk and to aid digestion.

In a table published by the British Horse Society, two to two and a half pounds of good hay equals one pound of oats in food value.

Beginning distance riders often ask for a feeding table that states the exact amounts of hay, concentrates, and supplements to be fed a novice horse who has been on pasture or in a box stall with little grain and little exercise. This is extremely difficult if not impossible in America because, as we have pointed out, there are different feed values in the various environments. However, the American Quarter Horse Association has funded research in equine nutrition, and if a person feels he must have something to go by, he might use the AQHA figures as a guideline.

If a horse is on a below-average pasture, he should be fed one and a half to two pounds of hay per 100 pounds of body weight. This is not a horse in training, but a horse that is standing around most of the time. It should also be noted that a horse on pasture, especially a lush, green pasture, will sweat more than a horse on dry feed.

A maintenance ration (daily) for a 1000-pound horse might be 16 pounds of hay (we prefer timothy) and 2 pounds of rolled oats. This is for the horse that is stabled or in a small area.

As training begins, the ratio of hay to oats should change, but decidedly not all at once — over a period of weeks. For instance, a 1000-pound animal who is being ridden one to three hours a day, which is defined as light work, might have a diet of fifteen pounds of timothy hay and three pounds of rolled oats. One pound of wheat bran and one pound of molasses might be added to this. When the horse progresses to a schedule of three to five hours of riding a day, the hay is cut down to ten pounds and the oats increased to six pounds. Longer and harder riding might merit a diet of ten pounds of timothy to six pounds of oats and six pounds of cracked corn.

Protein and carbohydrates are given in larger amounts as the work increases.

But again it should be emphasized that the horse must be considered as an individual. What is his age? What is his disposition?

The Flower Child, who was being trained for a 100-mile Endurance Ride, had a good appetite and good eating habits. He would chew for a while, look around, and then return to his hay. Tex gave him a two-pound can of oats to begin with, increasing it to six pounds a day. If Flower Child was fed too much grain, he became too "high," which meant the grain had to be adjusted so that he got enough to keep in condition but not so much that he became fractious. If that happened, he would wear himself out in the first part of the 100 miles by fighting to go. Tex was not going to try to win the Tevis or go for the Top Ten, only to complete the Ride.

Voodoo, who was being trained for a 35-mile Competitive Ride, is as lean by nature as Mazda is fat, and she received four pounds of oats a day. If she had more, she became nervous and thought she was a race-horse again. Scientifically, Voodoo's leanness could be explained by the fact that she had a higher metabolic rate than Mazda. When she was climbing or working hard, the metabolic rate went up, as it does with all horses, although to different degrees.

Mazda did well, to begin with, on hay and four pounds of grain, but Mazda does well on anything. Mazda, I decided, would be a back-up horse; that is, I would compete on him if something happened to Voo-doo. I would not ride him as regularly or as hard as the mare, but I would keep him in good shape for an emergency. Not infrequently a horse trained for weeks goes lame or sustains an injury or becomes ill and the rider has to drop out of the Rides he had hoped to enter, unless he has a second horse that he can use for competition.

Our program differed from that of some other experienced riders; indeed, the more riders there are, the more varied are the diets. Ruth Waltenspiel, winner of the NATRC President's Cup in 1974 (Competitive), used a mix of one-third by weight of rolled corn, oats, and barley; oat and alfalfa hay. Electrolytes were added to the grain on hot days to prevent dehydration. Most of this rider's competition occurred in California.

Another California rider, Bev Tibbitts, who also won the Cup, fed a mixture of chopped oat hay and alfalfa mixed with molasses, eight pounds twice daily. On harder than average work days, she fed one pound of mixed grains two times a day. A vitamin supplement was one tablespoon of a commercial liquid product twice daily. This was on a work schedule of one to three hours a day, four to five days a week.

An endurance rider who placed in the Top Ten in the Tevis fed, in addition to hay, good quality Omolene (Purina), bran, vitamins, salt, oats, and a hot linseed mash a couple of times a week. Supplementing this were Calf Manna (Albers), horse pellets, and carrots. The hay was fed on a basis of 16 pounds per 1000 pounds of horse, and the grain, at the start of training, 6 pounds. As the horse became better conditioned, the grain was increased to 14 pounds and the amount of hay lowered to 10 pounds.

For a military Endurance Ride in 1922, the horse was allowed an unlimited supply of hay, four pounds of grain in the morning, two pounds at noon, four pounds again in the later afternoon after the horse had been cooled off, and at eight o'clock in the evening, another four pounds. The hay fed was a ratio of four pounds of alfalfa to ten pounds of timothy.

On days that Bev Tibbitts did not ride her competitive horse, she did not feed grain. We cut the grain by two-thirds on days our horses were not ridden, which was usually one day a week. The British Horse Society suggests a bran mash for a horse that has been worked hard and then is at rest in the stable. As it happened, our horses were not confined to box stalls. When a horse is conditioned for only one Ride, and after that returns to being a pleasure animal, his customary diet can be resumed. When our horses are not being ridden they usually subsist on a diet of timothy hay, or they are put on a good pasture.

Overfeeding when a horse has been ridden hard and then left to do nothing in a stable or small pasture, and is then ridden again, can result in azoturia. In these cases, the muscles of the hindquarters and croup are involved. The circulation in the area cannot get rid of the products of metabolism, which build up in the muscles, causing stiffness and excruciating pain. A horse may start out normally, and then suddenly become stiff in the hindquarters and start to sweat profusely; if he urinates, the fluid will be darkish brown. In severe cases, the horse will collapse in the hindquarters and be unable to get up, and might eventually die.

The remedy is to dismount immediately, for exercise aggravates the condition. Trailer or truck the horse back to the stable and call a veterinarian who can give the horse an injection. Then feed the horse a bran mash with Epsom salts, and for as long a while as the veterinarian recommends, a small amount of hay and bran. If the attack is severe, the horse should not be ridden for some months; if mild, several weeks' rest is sufficient.

Founder or laminitis should also be a concern of the rider. It affects the distance horse if he is turned out in a rich pasture or fed heavily during periods of idleness. In addition, it can be caused by riding too long and too fast on hard roads, by drinking too much cold water, and, some authorities say, by standing in the cold and rain after a tiring journey in a truck or trailer. Acute laminitis can develop without warning and can be extremely painful. The laminae of the foot become inflamed and the bone as well may be involved. Laminitis usually affects the forefeet. In mild cases, the horse walks stiffly; in more severe cases, he may stand with his hind legs drawn beneath him to take the weight off the front feet, or he will want to lie down. The pulse may be rapid and the temperature elevated. The shoes should be removed and the animal given a purgative of Epsom salts in bran mash. If possible, the feet should be put in a hot bran poultice. However, it is safer to call a veterinarian as soon as laminitis is suspected. The veterinarian will probably recommend that, as the animal improves, he should stand in cold water or mud for several hours at a time.

Chronic laminitis can result from an acute attack and this can make an animal a doubtful prospect for distance riding.

It is interesting to note the treatment that Dr. J. K. Ward of Hamilton, Montana gives to some cases of laminitis, even to those so serious that the laminae have become separated and there is rotation of the third phalanx. A hardwood pattern is cut to fit the hoof and glued on with a special adhesive. This pattern is so shaped that the walls of the hoof are not allowed to touch the ground, which would increase the pain and pressure on the affected parts. In other words, the pressure is on the center of the hoof. Within six months or a year, horses treated in this fashion have grown new hoofs and apparently had no further problems.

In cases of mild laminitis, shoeing can sometimes solve the difficulty.

Anemia is another condition that may result from a faulty diet. Usually a horse shows it by a slowdown in his performance. When an owner notices that his horse tires easily and is losing his enthusiasm for being ridden, he should check the mucous membranes in the animal's mouth. If they are pale, the chances are that he is anemic. A blood test by a veterinarian will show if the blood count is low, and a supplementary diet will be recommended, as well as a test for parasites, for this last is another and frequent cause of anemia. Continued exercise of an anemic horse is not advisable, since it can damage the heart. Anemia among distance horses is not uncommon, and for that reason, many veterinarians check the gums when they first examine a horse.

A digestive disorder that every distance rider must watch out for is colic, which is evidenced by a swollen abdomen and severe pain. The horse paws the ground, tries to bite at his belly, breaks out in a cold sweat, groans, and attempts to lie down. Severe cases can result in death. Colic — that is, real colic and not the psychosomatic sort that Voodoo had when she was confined in a box stall — is caused by a number of things: by moldy hay, overfeeding a hard-worked horse, a sudden change in diet, too many green apples, too much cold water to drink when the horse is hot, or eating sand along with grass. A veterinarian should be called immediately; the sooner the horse is relieved of his pain, the better his chances of recovery. The horse should be kept walking, even when the pain — which is spasmodic — makes him want to roll. A veterinarian can recommend a remedy to keep in the medicine chest for emergencies.

Distance riders should also watch out for impaction, i.e., blockage of the large intestine by such roughage as alfalfa with large, hard stems, or any substandard hays. If a horse doesn't have enough water, he may be unable to digest correctly and may become constipated. In these cases, as in the others, it is best to call the veterinarian.

The only rules for feeding that might be generally applied are these:

Feed the best hay and grain available. This means do not buy dusty or moldy hay, and make sure that the grain is clean and, in the case of oats, that the kernels are full and firm.

Give a balanced ration.

Unless a person is experienced, he will do better to buy commercial feeds and supplements than to try to mix his own. There are many good ones on the market.

A diet that might do for one horse might not be suitable for another. A rider should learn to know what diet his horse requires.

Do not change the ration too quickly.

Do not work hard after a full feed.

Water the horse before feeding, and give him hay before he gets his grain.

Do not feed or water a horse until he has been cooled off after a hard day's work.

Tex and I fed hay often and in small amounts. Studies in nutrition financed by the American Quarter Horse Association and the Arabian Horse Registry of America show that frequent feedings aid the horse's digestion, which is not surprising, since in his natural state the horse grazes most of the time.

The stomach capacity of a horse is from eight to sixteen quarts for a full-grown animal, which is small compared to other herbivores and so designed that the stomach operates best on small amounts of food at frequent intervals. A horse's stomach empties completely in 24 hours if he is not fed; and when he is eating, food digests so quickly that hay eaten at the start of the meal goes into the intestine before the meal is finished.

Also, on occasion, we vary the feeding time by an hour so more. Knowing the horse is a creature of habit, we feel that if he misses a meal while being trailered to a Ride, or while he is on a Ride, he will not become upset at not receiving his oats exactly at a certain time. In other words, he has no definite minute-by-minute routine.

8. Mile After Mile of Trotting

ATHLETES are conditioned by exercise as well as diet, and this is true of the horse. No amount of vitamins, supplements, tranquilizers, or pain killers can get a horse that has not been correctly exercised through an Endurance Ride or a series of Competitive Rides. Unlike showing or racing, the stress is severe over a long period of time; either unsoundness will show up or the horse will be eliminated for fatigue.

To gauge the horse's performance, the owner should know the animal. We've said this before, and will say it again. What sort of disposition does the horse have? Is he calm and good-natured? Chunky in build? Or thin and nervous? What is the relationship between you and the horse? Have you ridden him on trails where he has learned to have confidence in you and you in him? Or have you only ridden in a ring or small area? Or is the horse new — will you have to become accustomed to one another?

There is an old German saying: "A horseman and his horse should be two hearts and one mind."

All this is important to the exercise program. The nervous horse will lose weight faster than the calm animal. The high-strung horse will be in danger of burning out where the stolid horse will not. Often a chunky horse climbs better than a long-legged, skinny type, but can't cover the ground as well on the level or at an extended trot.

These things will be learned by the beginner who is conditioning a horse for the first time, and by the experienced contestant who has a new mount.

In exercise, as in diet, moderation is the rule. No experienced contestant starts riding hard the day after the horse comes in from the pasture or out of the stable.

We might look first at the novice horse who is too fat and has never been on a distance Ride. Mazda, for instance. I had to lengthen the cinch to get the saddle on his back when I started riding him. For five or six days I rode for an hour at a walk and a trot, not for any certain distance or gait at certain times, but as I felt Mazda could go without tiring. Horses shouldn't feel pressure for distance riding; they should enjoy it. They should want to compete — not be made to compete. A tense, nervous rider will make his horse react in the same manner and both will tire.

The second week I lengthened the riding time to an hour and a half to two hours for five days a week, and as I did so, increased the amount of oats. The day I didn't ride I cut the grain ration and allowed Mazda to run in a pasture. If I hadn't had a pasture, I would have lunged him for a half hour on off days or ridden him a short distance. Occasionally I had to encourage Mazda, for he is inclined to be lazy, but as he lost weight and had more exercise, he became more animated. Sometimes I would stop, get off, and let him graze, but I never let him snatch at grass along the trail. We rode first on level ground and then in the hills so that Mazda could become accustomed to climbing and going down steep slopes, which I found he did not do well. Small, rolled caulks on the rear shoes helped somewhat, and Mazda improved with practice, but I knew he would never be as adept as some horses at going downhill, which meant that on a Ride I would lose time if much of a trail was steep. The Rides I hoped to enter were in the mountains and I trained with that in mind.

Every contestant should be informed about the sort of country in which he will be competing. Is the training area similar to the terrain where the Rides will take place? Will the Rides be mostly on the level? In sand? Rocky? Hot and humid or dry and cold? Often people forget that climate and altitude affect horses as well as humans. This does not mean that a person who hunts all winter around Middleburg will have difficulties if he enters the Virginia Ride at Hot Springs, which is in the foothills; this change of altitude is not drastic. Problems do occur when a horse is trained in a high, dry climate of the Rockies and is taken to a hot, humid area in Florida. Or if a horse comes from sea level to the Sierras. Or if a horse is accustomed to hard footing and encounters deep sand; or bushes and he sees cactus; or forest trails and he competes on paved roads. Or narrow tracks along the side of a mountain when he has only trotted on level, wide lanes. If a contestant arrives at a Ride a day ahead of an event, he can ride part of the trail. To cover it all he would need to come a week before, since he must not exhaust his horse by preliminary trials. The map furnished by the management and advice from other contestants is often sufficient information.

As far as altitude is concerned, a horse does better if he arrives from a low altitude to a high one (or the other way around) immediately before a Ride, or at least three weeks ahead of time. That is to say that, like humans, he needs time to become accustomed to the altitude, or he can manage if he has no chance to be affected within a 24-hour period.

Usually the beginner is not going to travel a thousand miles to a Ride; he will enter one in his vicinity, which is wise. Also, he should enter a Competitive Ride before trying an Endurance test. In the Competitive Ride he has time to realize the importance of small routines that must be considered in training, as well as the riding. One of these is teaching the horse to tie at night.

Some Rides provide box stalls, but others have no accommodations and the horses must be fastened to trailers or trucks. I had seen all manner of abuses in this respect — horses tied too short or too long, trailers not blocked, horses too close so that they could kick each other, horses tied to the rear of trailers where the doors banged against them. My first experiment was to tie Voodoo for a few hours to the side of the trailer (which I blocked) with enough rope so that she could move around, but not enough to get her foot through.

Mazda did not like being tied. He preferred a box stall. Nor did Flower Child or Voodoo enjoy being restricted to the side of a trailer, but gradually we got them accustomed to it.

Watering is important, too. Frequently horses will not drink in a strange place. In mountainous areas where there are plenty of streams this is not a problem, but in the southwestern deserts, in some parts of the Southeast where the water is brackish, and in California, which is semiarid, horses have to drink from buckets filled from a faucet. If they don't like the taste of the water, they won't drink it, which might mean dehydration. As a solution, a knowledgeable rider suggested putting a tablespoon of vinegar in the water early in training, so that the horse becomes accustomed to the vinegar and it flavors whatever he drinks.

Incidentally, vinegar has other uses. A friend told me that her horse was not bothered by flies when he had a tablespoon of vinegar a day, but that it had to be the old-fashioned kind with a "mother."

Yet another matter we considered during training was getting our horses accustomed to strange sights and sounds. We forded rivers, followed highways with cars speeding by, halted our horses near the tracks when trains were coming, trotted by the airfield when planes were landing. Our horses were exposed to sonic booms, peacocks, large pigs, and bulldozers. Voodoo snorted; Mazda did not turn a hair; nor did Flower Child. But all three had the screaming meemies when they saw the pony who was their constant companion pulling a cart.

Whenever we had time, we loaded the horses into a trailer and took them to country where they had not been before. People tend to train in their immediate area, with the result that the horse is suspicious when he goes on a Ride. A horse that will behave beautifully at home can become a terrified beast who will not leave the stable or trot in a straight line. The horse that is accustomed to a strange place and strange sights, to crowds of other horses and people, has a decided advantage on a Ride. He will relax and tend to business, while the nervous animal will waste time shying at spooks in the bushes.

After the first two weeks, when Mazda had begun to get into his stride, I estimated his speed at various gaits, which every contestant must do if he is to make a Ride in the required time. To do this, Tex and I and my friend Margit, who is a truly experienced horsewoman, measured a distance of a mile and timed ourselves at the three gaits for the stated distance with a stop watch. The speed of our three horses varied widely, as it does with all horses. The Flower Child and Margit's Hungarian had long, extended trots; Mazda could not keep up with them and I didn't try to make him. Voodoo, when I rode her, did better, but even she could not stay level with the other two. This did not greatly matter, for Tazilo, Margit's Hungarian, and the Flower Child were in training for the Tevis, while I intended to enter one 35-mile Ride.

The gaits are estimated at approximately these speeds:

The walk — 3 to 5 miles per hour.

The average trot — 7 to 10 miles per hour. This can vary from 12 to 30 miles per hour, the faster gait being that of a professional trotter, which does not concern distance riders.

The gallop — 12 to 20 miles per hour.

The run — 25 to 35 miles per hour.

Gaits vary according to the horse and the terrain. A horse can travel many miles at a trot because the diagonal support of this gait tires him less than the canter.

The extended trot is favored by most distance riders, and if a horse has not been trained to it, it is a good idea to get him accustomed to stretching out at that long, ground-devouring gait. To do this, encourage a horse to trot as fast as he can. When he breaks into a gallop, pull him in easily; then loosen the reins and get him to trot again. Gradually the horse will learn to reach out.

After the first few weeks, we rode from five to ten miles a day, and then I did 20 miles once a week with steep climbs. We did some galloping, too, but not for long periods. As most people are aware, galloping develops wind, while trotting legs up an animal and helps in gaining stamina. Endurance riders gallop more in training than Competitive contestants, since the former is a race while the latter is a timed event. Toward the end of training, I did 30 miles while Tex and Margit rode 50, rating their horses for speed and distance.

It is extremely difficult to lay out a timetable for training, since, as has been emphasized, every horse is different and so are the terrain, the climate, and the type of Ride. What may be good for one horse under certain circumstances might not do at all for another horse in another area. The rider must use his own judgment; indeed, the rider who knows when his horse is overtrained, too soft, or at his peak is the successful contestant. If he depends on charts to tell him what to do at a certain time, he will be in trouble. This is as true for the novice as it is for the advanced rider.

However, if a novice wants a guideline, he might be helped by knowing the schedule other riders have followed, and again we emphasize that even these riders vary their program. Suppose a horse were ridden some distance on a Sunday, either in a 30-mile Ride or for a 30-mile workout. The animal has not yet reached his peak but is in the middle of training. On Monday he might be ridden or trotted easily for three or five miles and then allowed to rest on Tuesday. On Wednesday he might have 8 to 12 miles' walking, trotting, and a short gallop. On Thursday he might be ridden approximately 13 miles, and on Friday be allowed to rest. On Saturday he might be ridden 20 miles and on Sunday from 25 to 30 miles.

Some contestants allow only one day of rest, some believe in three days with lunging and a short walk or trot of half an hour to keep the horse limber.

A horse that is stabled naturally needs more lunging and riding than a horse that is moving freely about in a pasture.

If a horse is allowed to rest on a Thursday, and is trailered a long distance to a Ride on Friday, he should be lunged or led about and allowed to graze or ridden a short distance so that he will not become stiff.

But keep in mind that the only way to develop a successful training program is by experience.

When we were training, I always kept in mind this definition of condition that I had read in a book on animal management published for the U.S. Cavalry School. Somehow or other, it gave me a clear picture of what I was aiming for and therefore made it easier to attain.

"Condition," the definition read, "means bodily health, muscular strength, and power of endurance sufficient to perform satisfactorily and without injury the work required."

On British Rides, which do not have the steep climbs that we have in the western part of the United States, the gait averages seven miles per hour. The majority of eastern Competitive Rides average approximately the same. For the Golden Horseshoe, the big British Endurance Ride of 50 miles the first day and 25 miles the second, the gait averages nine miles per hour. North American Trail Ride Conference Rides average five to six miles an hour, and Rocky Mountain and some Canadian Rides average 6½ to seven miles an hour.

At all times we watched our horses to see that they were not overtrained. A horse that becomes worn out from too much hard riding goes off his feed, is cranky, and is reluctant to start in the morning. In the case of a Competitive horse, overtraining is not so much of a problem, unless he is campaigned every weekend. The Competitive horse is not ridden as fast or as far as the Endurance horse in training, nor is he fed such large amounts of grain.

According to Dave Nicholson, a top Competitive trail rider, if a person is competing in a season of NATRC Rides, a well-conditioned horse can do 60 miles each weekend and not be unduly stressed. In this case, during the week, a two-mile gallop on two days would be sufficient to keep the horse in shape, or a four-mile trot on a Tuesday and Thursday. However, a horse would be taxed considerably beyond his strength to compete in an Endurance Ride every weekend.

When we were training, we did not ride on Sundays and allowed the horses to rest a day before we trailered them to a Ride.

Don't, advises Nicholson, try to keep the horse at peak condition over a long season. The best way to avoid this is not to attempt to win every event a person enters, but to compete to the best of one's ability. The distinction is a fine one. For the person who enters one 35-mile Ride or a three-day 100-mile Ride, the problem is not difficult. For the person who campaigns for a season, it is something that must be considered seriously. Only experience and knowledge of the individual horse can tell a contestant when his animal is in top shape. Indeed, there lies the secret of the successful and the unsuccessful distance rider.

A word of caution. Not only beginners but experienced contestants often enter too many events so that the horse becomes exhausted halfway through the season. Time after time, the judges see horses that have been over-ridden, whose hip bones protrude, who stare with lackluster eyes and move reluctantly, or, while not so obviously tired, are still worn out. These horses place lower on each succeeding Ride, go lame, become permanently disabled, or die.

Never, never should a horse be ridden to exhaustion in one Ride or a succession of Rides.

Later we will discuss how veterinarians judge for signs of fatigue, but there is one way of testing condition that every person should know as soon as he starts training, and that is by taking the temperature, pulse, and respiration. TPR's are taken on every Ride and are one of the most important factors in evaluating a horse's performance. If an animal's pulse is above normal and does not have a satisfactory rate, the horse is not properly conditioned. If the pulse should continue high, the horse is not suited to distance riding. A rapid pulse can be a sign of illness or that the horse is being pushed too hard. Another sign of trouble is a temperature that is below normal, or one that is unusually high. Equally significant is abnormal respiration that could be symptomatic of thumps, a condition that is seen in severely fatigued horses where the flanks go in and out convulsively.

The last few years, the temperature has not been taken as regularly as it was in the past, the veterinarians feeling it is unnecessary and time-consuming where the horses are not unduly stressed or in obvious trouble. Nevertheless, the temperature is important and a person training a horse for distance riding should know how to take it and how to read it.

A horse's normal temperature ranges between 100° and 101° F, although it can be as low as 98° and as high as 104° after climbing a hill on a hot afternoon. Temperatures vary according to the weather and the time of day, but if the temperature of a healthy horse gets above 104°, the rider is probably overtaxing his animal. A temperature above 106° signifies an emergency.

To take a temperature, it is necessary to use a thermometer similar to those used by humans, but slightly larger and made so that a string can be tied to the end. The reason for this is that if the horse's muscles contract and the thermometer is drawn into the rectum, the string will serve to pull it out. Put a little grease on the bulb (sometimes we spit on it) and, standing to one side, lift the horse's tail and insert the thermometer in the rectum. After two minutes, it can be removed and read.

The pulse, like that of humans, can be taken with or without a stethoscope. Mine I carried in a leather case on my saddle. The best advertisement for a stethoscope is that veterinarians carry them on Rides and don't waste time trying to take the pulse by other means. The two ear pieces can be adjusted doctor fashion, and the small circular piece placed on the horse's body behind the elbow. At rest, the horse's heart has a slow, regular rhythm — ker-plunk, ker-plunk. The ker-plunk is counted as one beat, not two, which confuses those who are unaccustomed to taking PR's. Once in a while a horse will have a faster pulse than usual, or a different rhythm. On one Ride where I was a lay judge, a contestant brought a veterinary certificate testifying that her horse had an irregular heartbeat, but that it had never bothered the animal. We allowed the horse to compete, which he did, suffering no ill effects.

But we do not always have a stethoscope, so it is advisable to be able to tell the pulse without one. The pulse can be detected in four places on the horse's body. The first is by the artery on the inside of the jawbone, which is best found by feeling with the fingertips along this area until the arterial beat is located. Another pulse is in the groove in the tail near the root; a third, the digital pulse, can be felt below the fetlock just lateral to the flexor tendon; and the fourth is in the chest.

Experienced contestants can guess how their opponents are doing by watching the pulse beat in an opposing horse's chest after a steep climb. Only practice can make this easy.

Taking a pulse requires a watch with a second hand. The heartbeat can be counted for fifteen seconds and then multiplied by four, which gives the pulse for one minute. The average pulse at complete rest, according to B. C. Throgmorton, D.V.M., of Gilroy, California, who is one of the most knowledgeable judges of Distance Rides, varies between 28 and 40. Influencing this are the age, breed, and condition of the horse, and the environment. A horse will naturally have a lower pulse at home than in a strange place surrounded by other horses. Also, if a horse is well-conditioned, his pulse should be lower than that of the poorly conditioned animal.

If a horse, while exercising, has a heart rate between 60 and 65, he is in good shape. Mazda's pulse after climbing a small hill was 60, but unfortunately he arrived at the top some distance behind Flower Child, who went up with long, determined strides.

Checking respiration soon becomes routine and can be done in the saddle by looking at the horse's sides, or by standing behind the horse and watching the flanks move in and out. Another way is to hold a hand to the horse's nostrils. At rest, respiration averages between 7 and 25 breaths per minute; a few counts one way or the other makes no difference. Should the respiration be above 55 at rest, there might be difficulties. Gasping and heaving after a climb and continuing to do so is a bad sign. A healthy horse will, when he reaches the top of a hill, stand heaving for a few seconds, then draw a deep breath and resume normal breathing.

Veterinarians are quick to point out that PR's are not the sole criteria for judging a horse's condition. Other factors are important, such as dehydration, lameness, and fatigue. Initial readings when a horse checks in are not, according to some veterinarians, significant unless further readings are taken during the Ride, particularly recovery rates, which are calculated from the pulse and respiration taken immediately the horse arrives at a checkpoint, and again ten or fifteen minutes later. Longer than that, the PR's of a healthy horse will go down to near normal.

For a while it was felt that the horse with the lowest pulse was the best conditioned, but this theory has been modified. A Thoroughbred might have a high reading which shows not that he is poorly conditioned, but that he is exerting himself with the nervous tension typical of the breed. The recovery rate (considering the horse) is what counts.

Studies of judges' sheets and performance charts are informative. For instance, an Endurance Ride chart (see Appendix) explains why some horses were eliminated after a long, rigorous trail and others did well.

Keep in mind when reading the chart that the horse's normal pulse is between 28 and 40 and respiration from 7 to 40, depending on the animal. Naturally, a horse is not going to have those low rates at the checks on an Endurance Ride, but the veterinarians consider that if a horse's PR's fall to a safe count within fifteen minutes, he can be allowed to go on. If a horse has a pulse rate above 72, veterinarians do not like to let him continue, for they know he is too stressed for more work.

On this chart, the first horse came in at the checkpoint (where the veterinarians inspect the horse to make sure he is fit to continue) with a pulse of 120 and a respiration of 110. Since this was dangerously high and the horse so exhausted that he had thumps, he was eliminated.

The second horse came in with a respiration of 80 and a pulse of 120.

After one hour, the respiration had fallen to 22, but the pulse was 80, which was above the safety count, so this horse was eliminated as having poor recovery, a sign that he was becoming overstressed.

On the other hand, a horse that did extremely well came in with a pulse of 80, and after an hour had a pulse of 56. The respiration was 44 in, and out it was 18.

A second horse in good condition came in with a pulse of 88, and after an hour, had a pulse of 60. The respiration in was 80, and out was 32.

A danger signal to watch for is an inversion, which veterinarians define as a condition where the respiration rate is higher than the pulse rate. If neither the pulse nor the respiration is unduly elevated, the condition is not worrisome, but when a veterinarian sees a pulse of 85 and a respiration of 90, which is a 1:1 ratio, he may feel a horse should be eliminated if other problems of recovery are noted.

On Endurance Rides, as we pointed out, the readings are apt to be higher and the veterinarians stricter about eliminating marginal horses than they are on Competitive Rides, for the pace is faster and the distance greater.

It is interesting to note that in areas where Competitive Rides were held for a number of years, the readings were higher in the first Rides than in latter events, which suggests that the riders learned how to condition their horses.

Through the woods. *Peterson*

Ruth Waltenspiel on her champion Arab; Kandar, ridden over 1000 miles in one year of competitive trail riding. 1974 winner of the NATRC President's cup. *Kim Hutchison*

The down hill trot. Margit Bessenyey at the Virginia 100 Mile Competitive Trail Ride. *I. Haas*

The veterinary judges. *Peterson*

Alexander Mackay-Smith as lay judge.
Ernst Peterson

A PR girl takes a pulse.
Peterson

The preliminary check at a trail ride. *Hughes*

Weighing in. *Peterson*

Linda Tellington on Hungarian Warrior at the Virginia 100 Mile Competitive Trail Ride. *I. Haas*

The distance rider stands in her stirrups. Linda Peters on three-quarter Arabian Dagger.

Tex Johnson on the Tevis Cup Ride.

A scene on a western trail ride. *Ernst Peterson*

Margit Bessenyey on Hungarian Jegyes
at the Virginia 100 Mile Competitive
Trail Ride. *Ira Haas*

Casey, grade horse who was three times National Champion of the NATRC and 1971 winner of the President's Cup at age 14. At age 15, he placed in the Top Ten at the Tevis. Owned and ridden by Bev Tibbitts.

9. The Tricks of Training

THE HORSES we were training were over five years old, that age, as mentioned, being the youngest a horse is allowed to compete in the majority of Distance Rides. The rule is nearly universal, and for a good reason. A horse under five is not mature and the strain on tendons and tissues in the legs can cause irreparable damage.

On our ranch years ago, horses were not started under saddle until three, and were considered immature until they were five. Every conscientious horseman realized that a horse under three was similar to a child of ten or twelve — he simply did not have his growth and so could not travel long distances carrying weights without creating problems in the future, if not at the time.

Since then we have learned more about the strain on ligaments and tendons when the horse's foot hits the ground, and why the strain is particularly damaging to immature animals, although the principle applies to horses of all ages.

If a horse is tired or out of condition, the muscles, as in humans, do not draw as they should and undue strain is put on the tendons and ligaments, sometimes causing a sprain or rupture.

According to Dr. B. C. Throgmorton, an astonishing number of leg problems are caused by too early training. Some of these are bowed tendons, sesamoid fractures, ringbone, and navicular bursitis. Anyone who wants proof of this has only to visit a racing stable on a third-rate circuit and see the legs of the horses who have been blistered and fired, or who will have to be destroyed because they have broken down completely. In racing and showing, economics dictates training the young horse, for every year a horse is fed, stabled, and cared for increases the bill.

The cost of raising a distance horse is infinitesimal compared to that of raising a Derby hopeful, but it is nevertheless a factor to be considered

HOW TO RIDE UPHILL

from a monetary view. If money is a consideration, the novice would do better to buy an older sound horse, say from seven to ten, than a three-year-old that he would have to break, feed, and stable for two years before he could enter in competition.

Mile after mile of trotting can put a terrific strain on a horse's legs, which is the reason the animal must, in addition to being sound, be conditioned. When we trotted, we kept that gait for long distances, rather than slowing to a walk, trotting again, then slowing. A continued extended trot creates a rhythm between horse and rider, is less tiring (with practice), and covers ground.

HOW NOT TO RIDE UPHILL

On Distance Rides, trotting is not confined to the level. In order to make time on many Competitive Rides and most Endurance Rides, the contestant must trot down all but the steepest hills. In Endurance Rides, contestants sometimes dismount and lead their horses at a fast gait down the switchbacks in order to save their strength, but this demands hours of jogging on foot and a strong constitution. For this reason some Endurance riders wear tennis shoes. On an Endurance Ride, a contestant cannot afford to walk downhill — he must run; but a Competitive rider is seldom under such pressure and can remain mounted.

Many Competitive Rides do not allow the contestant to get out of the saddle while in forward motion. However, at one time or another, a contestant will have to lead his horse downhill and he should learn to do so without the animal threatening to go over him or forcing him to slide down a cliff faster than he would like. One method of accomplishing this is to carry a stick or long crop horizontally at an angle between rider and horse, to serve as a barrier. If the horse starts to come down too fast, the rider should stop, emphasize the stick or crop as a barrier by holding it between himself and the animal, and then proceed at a slower pace, increasing the gait when the horse learns to keep his distance.

Now for a word of caution. A novice in the saddle should not trot down a steep hill; he should walk and make up time by an extended trot on the level. Unless the horse and rider know what they are doing, the horse might stumble. Indeed, it is more difficult to go downhill than it is to go up, and the beginner should practice at every opportunity. First, he should find out how his horse travels naturally on a grade, for some horses are more agile in this respect than others. One expert insists it is because of the conformation of the hocks. I don't know, but Mazda went downhill like an old woman in high-heeled shoes, and even after months of training he was not at ease on a slope. Voodoo was more agile, while Tazilo and the Flower Child were adept. In the beginning we trotted slowly down easy grades, then at a faster gait, and after a few weeks we practiced on steep hills. The secret is to remain relaxed and to encourage the horse to be relaxed, too. Man and animal must have confidence in each other. The rider must not stiffen or jerk at the reins if the trail becomes littered with rocks or drops into a gully. I learned this years ago when we rounded up horses on the range. The herd would take off at a dead run across the prairie and down the side of the mountain, swerving through timber and dodging rocks, and we, on our horses, close behind. If I kept in mind the picture of those horses racing down the side of the mountain, I had trust in the ability of my animal to negotiate difficult places. The horse is a footsure animal unless he has been spoiled by man or lived all his life on level ground. In that case, a person should trailer his horse to the nearest hills once a week, or, if that is impossible, find something to go up and down, even if it is only a borrow pit. Better still, the rider should take care to enter Rides that are not in rough country.

Above all, he should not try to play cowboy down a steep hill unless he really is a cowboy or a very experienced Endurance contestant. Nor should he overdo downhill training, or he will have a lame or sore-footed horse.

Another trick that is used more often in Endurance riding than in Competitive Rides is tailing; that is, the rider dismounts and grabs his horse's tail to be pulled up a hill, thus saving the horse by getting the rider's weight off his back, but, at the same time, keeping control of the animal and using him to assist the rider in negotiating the steep slope. I have seen riders hanging onto their horses' tails and the horses climbing upward without guidance. Another method is a drive line on one side that with practice can be used to rein the horse by pulling on one side or drawing it against the neck when the horse is to go in the opposite direction. The line can be a light piece of rope that is kept coiled on the saddle. While the rider is hanging onto the tail, he can direct his horse by the makeshift rein at the same time.

Tailing, also, must be practiced, first by getting the horse accustomed to having someone pull on his tail, and to traveling with his rider on the ground at his rear. A horse that kicks or tries to run is a handicap.

When trotting, the experienced distance rider, bent slightly forward, stands in the stirrups, which are longer than what he might use ordinarily. His legs are directly under him, his weight on the balls of his feet, a position that can be adapted to either a western or English saddle, and that saves the horse from a sore back. The rider's center of gravity is over that of the horse. Jockeys and jumpers aid their horses in this manner, and distance riders have found it is helpful to their horses to do the same. If balance is a problem, the rider can brace himself with the palm of his hand on the pommel. Learning to do this properly is hard work, and may cause aching muscles in the legs, but it will pay off in the condition of the horse in a Ride.

Interestingly enough, the old-time cowboys often stood to the trot, holding on to the pommel with one hand. Only later did it become popular in western pleasure classes to sit the trot. If a person tried this on a Distance Ride, he would be shaken to a jelly and his horse would be so tender about the spine he would be unable to move.

Most riders know that going uphill they should stand in the stirrups and lean forward, and that if they do post to the trot, as many do, they should change diagonals every once in a while.

Tex and Margit rode together because their horses matched stride for stride. I rode behind on Voodoo, which did not bother me. Several times I turned off and took a different trail to accustom Voodoo to leaving her friends, for nothing is more aggravating than to ride a herd-bound horse on a Ride, and yet people come up to me frequently as a judge to ask, "Can I start with so-and-so? Our horses are used to going together and we'll have trouble if they're separated."

These people do not stop to think that one horse is apt to be faster than another, so that he has to be held back; or one horse might fall out during the Ride and the other will have to proceed, which he will do, neighing and looking around for his pal instead of paying attention to business.

The steady trot, mile after mile, that demands such stamina is the reason that size has little to do with the performance of a distance horse. A small, tough animal that can carry weight can outdo a large horse that cannot hold the gait. An added advantage of the small horse is his agility. Indeed, many experts feel that a horse over 15.3 has a handicap, which seems to be proved by the size of the Endurance and Competitive horses who have won and placed not only in the United States but in Canada, England, and Australia.

Over the years, contestants have learned a number of equestrian skills, some new, some centuries old. One of these is the importance of rhythm. To demonstrate — gallop a horse up a hill, letting him choose his own pace. The gait will coordinate with the breathing, so count in rhythm, 1...2...3...4, 1...2...3...4. At the top of the hill, which should be level, change to a trot and continue counting. After one or two times, the horse will learn to breathe in coordination to the trot, as he did to the uphill gallop. This rhythm of breathing and action is employed by athletes, and on a Distance Ride, a horse is an athlete. This takes practice; a novice should not expect to do it the first time he attempts it.

When we began training, our horses naturally sweated heavily. The sweat was soapy, particularly on the flanks and the edges of the saddle blanket, but after a few weeks, the sweat became clear and had a good, healthy odor. The horses never stopped sweating entirely, and if they had, we would have been concerned, since a horse, like a human, not only cools himself but gets rid of body wastes by sweating.

How much a horse should sweat and the type of sweat are questions debated by judges and riders; much of it depends on the horse, the type of feed he's had, the climate, and the stress. On a Canadian Ride, a contestant, interestingly enough, told a veterinarian judge that an old trick was to taste a horse's sweat, and if was strongly acid, the horse was not in condition. In Europe these tricks are attributed to the gypsies, and in North America to the Indians.

Once the horses were in shape, we emulated, as closely as possible, Ride procedures, which meant for one thing that we watched our riding time by checking ourselves in at the start, at various stops, and at the finish.

Some people have no problem with riding time, but others, of whom I am one, are confused by estimating speed versus mileage, and for that reason, we might go into it in detail. Actually it is not difficult. The maps furnished by the management show the distance and the type of terrain, while the entry blanks give riding time, which is repeated at the briefing the night before the Ride. For this example, let us say the Ride is a Competitive Ride of 35 miles, to be ridden in six to six and one-half hours, which means the rider will have to average five miles an hour on his horse, or a little less if he considers the half-hour leeway. On this Ride, time is not taken out for the veterinary fifteen-minute checks on the trail, or for the one-hour lunch stop. However, some Rides do subtract the lunch stop and some check stops from riding time, so the contestant must know the rules before he leaves the starting gate.

The Ride begins at seven o'clock, which means the contestant cannot come in before 2:30, the two fifteen-minute check stops and the one-hour lunch stop being added to the five hours on the trail. Many riders keep this overall riding time on one wristwatch. On the other watch, they keep their actual riding time; that is, the time spent on the trail minus lunch and checks. Thus, if he walks on an uphill climb, he knows he must trot or gallop on the level (preferably an extended trot) to make up for lost time; if he finds himself five miles from the finish with three-quarters of an hour still left, he must slow down. However, if he has rated himself correctly, he should not be in the latter situation. On the other hand, if he has been riding at less than five miles an hour, he must increase his speed, remembering that he has a half-hour leeway. If he comes in too soon on a Competitive Ride, he is penalized. He is also penalized if he comes in after the half-hour leeway. Most riders come in between the hour and the half-hour.

Not only did practicing riding time give us experience in rating our horses, but it emphasized the importance of every turn of the second hand on our wristwatches. Adjusting the saddle blanket or looking at the horse's shoe, visiting with friends or admiring the view meant minutes that had to be accounted for. Lost riding time is doubly important, because it increases the difficulty of keeping an even pace. Naturally, going down steep hills or fording streams or climbing, the horse has to walk, but the experienced competitor allows for this and can still make up time by the extended trot on easier parts of the trail; but if he has four or five minutes to make up that he didn't anticipate, his timing is off and he'll only exhaust himself and the horse if he tries to recover those minutes by galloping wildly along the trail. An easy, cadenced pace, whether five or nine miles an hour, will bring the best results.

Our noon lunch stop was in the hills where Margit had constructed a number of corrals. The grass, which was timothy mixed with clover and wildflowers, grew knee-high; pines shaded a picnic area for the riders near a small stream that burbled among willows. Since the horses were on hay and the grass was rich enough to cause founder, the horses were only allowed to graze a short time; nor were they permitted more than a few swallows from the creek after they had been cooled off, for the water was achingly cold. On the trail we let them have five or six swallows from streams or whatever water was available, to prevent dehydration and cramps. A little water at intervals maintains the body fluids and prevents a frantic animal from wanting to gulp water at the finish. How many horses, dehydrated and exhausted, have developed colic because they drank too fast and too much at the end of the day!

Our noon stop was an hour, which gave us time to feed a flake of hay if the horses wanted it, which they usually did. A horse that eats, drinks, and urinates naturally is relaxed, but if the horse is tense, it helps to lead him away from the others and encourage him to graze. For some, this is sufficient, but others need a sponging with lukewarm water on the face and on the legs. Under no condition dump a bucket of cold water on a hot horse, for this can cause muscle contractions and pneumonia. Blanketing, sponging, and bathing depend on the weather. If it is cold, a horse shouldn't be wet all over with water, but sponged on the face and legs, blanketed, and led around until cooled off. On the other hand, if the weather is hot and dry, a warm water sponging all over will make a horse feel better. Actually, the best guide is to treat the horse as one would oneself, and don't fuss too much. Every Ride has contestants who are perpetually busy with buckets, brushes, and other paraphernalia. If the blanket is on, they take it off; if the horse is tied, they untie him, when all the poor animal wants is to be left alone.

At the noon stop we loosened the cinches, but left the saddles on, while we walked the horses around to cool them off. When it was cold or raining, we added a blanket over the horse, but still didn't take the saddle off, for removing the saddle too quickly can cause heat bumps, which look like bug bites and are caused by the blood rushing back into the area where circulation has been restricted by the weight of the rider and saddle. Ice reduces heat bumps, but since it is seldom available, a gentle massage can often restore normal circulation.

Many problems can be avoided by walking the last few miles to the finish line and by coming into noon stops and checkpoints at a slow gait.

This includes steep climbs, which the horse can take by easy stages rather than by plunging wildly upward. Moderation in this respect will mean lower PR's and more points from the judges for the contestant's riding ability.

But what if the horse's respiration is still high at a checkpoint? Went and Linda Tellington, who in 1966 wrote one of the first manuals on Endurance and Competitive trail riding recommended leading the horse around fairly fast to correspond with his breathing, then decreasing the gait as the breathing slows down. Eventually the horse, unless he is in real trouble, will take the all-important deep breath and his breathing will be restored to normal. In my own experience, I have found that merely leading the horse around at some distance from the others brought the desired results, although this is not always possible on a ten-minute check where horses, contestants, PR teams, veterinary judges, and spectators are jammed on a narrow trail.

Not much can be done on a ten-minute check to lower a pulse that is too high. Again, isolation and leading around sometimes are effective. On a longer check, the Tellingtons suggested massage over the hips and forearms with a circular motion in the direction of the heart, and locking the fingers behind the tendons in the cannon area, rubbing upward. "Within five minutes you will have gained control of the pulse."

Some veterinarians doubt if this is possible, and say that the pulse will go down with rest unless the horse has serious problems.

On occasion, a horse will come in with an elevated temperature. As any mother who has cared for a feverish child knows, the treatment is simple. No aspirin for the horse, nor alcohol rub, but if the weather is hot and dry, the horse's head can be covered with damp cloths and his legs sponged with cool water. Should the weather be cold and wet, the horse may be covered with a waterproof blanket and wiped dry beneath it.

What if the horse starts to stiffen after he's arrived at a noon stop? Lead him around until time to start. When the Ride is over and before curfew, when no contestants are allowed in the stalls, massage his legs.

"Cold water and vigorous massage will keep a set of legs under a horse even after they start to go bad," Captain H. N. Beeman, Veterinary Corps, wrote after an Army Endurance trial.

Massage to relieve muscle and tendon stiffness is most effective when done by hand rubbing, which must always be directed toward the heart. The circulation will then return new blood to the parts of the body.

The legs should be rubbed upwards only, with the hands locked together behind the leg tendons, the heels of the hands moving up from the pasterns to the knee, with firm pressure to relieve filling or soreness. When the lower legs have been attended to, the upper legs should be rubbed with the heel of the hand in a circular motion toward the heart. Then the shoulder, quarters, and neck, where the muscles frequently knot with fatigue. The back can be massaged on both sides with the heel of the hand, while the crest of the neck can be pinched between the heel of the hand and the fingers to loosen the muscles, but too much pressure should not be exerted on the withers where the bone projects.

If a horse is not accustomed to massage, start quietly, then gradually increase the pressure.

When Tex rode Voodoo in the Bitterroot Ride, she massaged the mare after completing the 40 miles the first day. Since I was one of the directors of the Ride, I could not help her, so I stood at some distance watching Tex in the box stall. It was dark and cold and Tex was as stiff and as tired as Voodoo. Wasn't it ridiculous that she should be working on a dumb horse instead of being in bed with a hot pad? Or at least in a bathtub foaming with Epsom salts? Our non-horsy friends might be right; this sort of thing could be carried too far. Then I thought of the months of training we'd devoted to Voodoo and our pride in her conditioning. Damn it, the beast had better be in shape to continue the next morning. And she would be. When Tex had brought her in, she had been stiff, bad-tempered, and tense. Now I could see in the semidarkness that she was beginning to relax.

Tex laughed, "Do you hear her groaning and sighing? She does it every time I pop a knot out of a muscle."

Before long, Voodoo was asleep.

In the morning, Voodoo was her customary self, and after doing another twenty miles, placed well in the lightweight division.

This does not mean that massage is a cure-all for fatigue, but that it might be beneficial in certain situations.

10. Ride Hard and Clean Tack

In our zeal for the horse, we sometimes forget the rider, which is an error, for a champion horse cannot go far unless his rider is in good physical shape, is well equipped, knows what he is doing, and is competitive. The last does not imply the rider should set out to win every event, but that he should have confidence in himself and a desire to do his best.

"The Ride," wrote Capt. H. N. Beeman of an Army Endurance trial, "demands excellent physical condition on the part of the rider, and to obtain this he must ride hard and live cleanly."

The latter piece of advice is a charming anachronism, but translated to mean good nutrition, rest, and exercise, it is as sound today as it was forty years ago.

Horse and rider work together, so why neglect one partner for the other?

As a judge, spectator, and contestant, I have seen veterinarians and PR teams converge on the horses and ignore the individuals in the saddles, which is natural, since it is the officials' job to rate the horses and not the riders, who are supposed to take care of themselves.

However, not all riders are capable of doing so. They might be physically but not emotionally prepared, or they might have the right mental attitude but not the strength. They do not pause to consider that what applies to the horse, applies to the rider.

The Fitzgeralds, Tevis Cup winners, are quoted in the *Arabian Horse News* as saying that many people become discouraged because of lack of preparation and of knowledge of what is expected of them.

"It is of the utmost importance that both horse and rider are prepared, have knowledge of the course and problems that will arise."

Anyone familiar with distance riding can cite numerous examples of failure to heed the Fitzgeralds' advice.

For instance, the woman who had trained horses for years and prided herself on her ability as an equestrienne; she had no doubt she could do a Competitive Ride easily, but at the noon lunch stop she collapsed beneath a tree, moaning, "I can't go on; I'm exhausted."

I sympathized with her, knowing that her every muscle ached, her legs felt like rubber, and her brain felt stuffed with cotton wool. While a friend led her horse around, we encouraged her to continue with the Ride, and being a good sport, she did so, but at the finish she admitted to me that she had no idea a Competitive Ride could be so difficult.

She had not bothered to find out that she would have to ride a steady, extended trot and that maintaining that gait for miles over trails and up and down hills is far more difficult than hunting or driving cattle or galloping around a ring. In addition, she did not really know what a mile was; many people don't. They speak glibly of having ridden or hiked so many miles, when actually they have covered less than half the distance. The measured miles on authorized Rides turn out to be much longer than the novice has imagined.

Carelessness is another fault. On one Ride I saw a pretty girl who was so busy chatting with a handsome drag rider that she missed a turn as broad as an interstate highway. There is nothing wrong about riding with another person if both pay attention to the trail, and if the horses trot at the same pace. The best companions don't chatter, and anyhow, who wants to shout to a rider ahead on the trail or behind, when riding at a fast trot?

A type more commonly found in the Midwest and West than in the East is the rider, usually a young man, who whoops and hollers on the trail, gallops up behind the other riders, and tries to spook the girls' horses. He is playing cowboy and is usually eliminated by the noon stop, where his horse arrives exhausted by his antics. He would not have completed the Ride under any circumstances, because he did not bother to condition his horse. To him a Ride is a spree, like a rodeo.

Juniors can also be monsters. On one Ride, the Juniors left after the Lightweights, of which I was a member. Shortly after we left the starting line, the Juniors passed us like a tornado, and were not seen until the lunch stop.

"Ten years is too young to ride forty miles!" a spectator exclaimed.

"Our ten-year-olds," I said, "with a few exceptions, are tougher than the adults. You can hardly drag them off their horses when the Ride is over."

The North American Trail Ride Conference and the Rocky Mountain Trail Ride Association allow ten-year-olds, while the Eastern Competitive Trail Ride Association limits Juniors to twelve years of age, and on the longer Rides, they must be accompanied by a responsible adult. In Virginia, Juniors must be eighteen years old and are limited to the 50-Mile Ride.

This is not to say that some Juniors are not responsible competitors; I have seen many who shame people three times their age.

Contestants who are ignorant or careless, or hope to gain an advantage over an opponent, are a menace on the trail. Passing another rider and then slowing down is a discourtesy. So, too, is refusing to allow a rider to go by if his horse is obviously the faster and the trail is wide. Shaking a hat or crop in front of a horse's face, or creating a disturbance which alarms the horses, are also thoughtless.

Fortunately these contestants are the exception, not the rule. The over-whelming majority are considerate of their horses and of other riders, for they are amateurs and no money is involved. What happens on Rides in California and Nevada that give large cash prizes is difficult to say. Even the Olympic riders admit that whan a gold medal is at stake, a rider will push his horse beyond what he might otherwise, or will take advantage of an opponent in a situation where he might not ordinarily. Substitute ten thousand dollars for a gold medal and an Endurance rider for the Olympic contender. To some competitors this heightens the challenge; it certainly makes the event more exciting to the spectators.

The people who win consistently in the Endurance Rides with cash prizes are professionals who have an incentive to train like a boxer or pro football player, while contestants who compete in Rides that award tro-phies or ribbons do so only from an appreciation of the sport. But some-times their enthusiasm wanes. The most common reason for not finish-ing or placing is the contestant's failure to train himself and his horse. He might lack the time or he might think he can get by with cutting cor-ners. If the Ride is not severe and the judges not as alert as they should be, he might do all right the first Ride, but his luck will not continue; nor should it.

Then there is the contestant who brings an obviously unsound horse to a Ride and is eliminated before the start. The contestant might not know that his horse has laminitis or a mild case of influenza, or he might sus-pect it and still hope to evade the judge's sharp eyes, which he will not. Elimination at the start is a disappointment when a person has hauled a horse for many miles and planned on the Ride for months; it is almost a tragedy when the unsound animal belongs to a Junior who prizes the old nag as the most wonderful horse in the world, and who fights back the tears at the judge's decision.

Contestants who train at home and never take their horse elsewhere are another problem. They, like their horses, are apt to be nervous in new territory. Dr. H. Hediger, Director of the Zürich Zoological Gardens, in his book, *The Psychology and Behavior of Animals in Zoos and Circuses,* describes the craving of horses for their stables as spatial attachment manifested to a great extent in wild animals; less so in domestic animals. People, Dr. Hediger feels, like animals, are divided into those who enjoy strange places and those who feel secure only at home. When both rider and horse belong to the latter group, problems can arise. The rider's apprehension hinders him in his ability to handle emergencies; he doesn't know how to get through swamps or cross narrow trails on shale rock, or ford fast rivers, and his nervousness communicates itself to the horse, so that the animal shies or loses its head.

The rider should be relaxed and yet alert to the trail and to his horse. He must be aware of a loose shoe, lameness, colic, and signs of fatigue; he must keep track of his riding speed and watch for trail markers. He can't do this if he is tired or has a headache or stomach cramps or blisters on his bottom and legs.

"The tired horse," Captain Beeman wrote, "needs support, and it is surprising how a rider can gather them up and carry them along with the legs. They seem to fall apart when one relaxes and lets go. All tired horses seem to lose that nicety of coordination in the hind quarters first, and this is particularly noticeable going downhill; it required more care and effort to guide them downhill than any other time."

An exhausted rider cannot dismount and run downhill as many do on Endurance Rides, nor can he tail a horse up a cliff. Nor would he be able, as a lieutenant did on a 150-mile Endurance Ride, to slit his boots from his swollen legs and lead his tired horse, so that after a rest at the checkpoint, the animal and rider were allowed to continue.

Gen. Earl D. Thomas, U.S. Cavalry, wrote:

"Everyone knows that it requires no special skill to ride a horse in such a way that he will break down or die. The better bred the horse, the more likely is this to happen, as a poor horse will give up long before he is in danger of such an ending. Only a well-bred horse will answer every call his rider may make on him. A good rider is expected to do more than ride his horse. He must nurse his horse and look after him with the greatest amount of thoughtfulness and bring into practice all of his experience and intelligence in the care of his mount. Individual practice alone will teach a man how to cover long distances in as short a time as possible without unnecessarily fatiguing his horse. A few failures will impress upon him the fact that a horse is not merely a machine that will go on forever at every pace, provided he is supplied with fuel.''

Some people are naturals for distance riding. They have the stamina of astronauts and unfailing vitality, and they thrive on competition. Whether this is significant or not, I don't know, but the women have round faces and strong thighs; they are outgoing and capable and they do not become tense during a Ride; they enjoy it.

When the military selected competitors for endurance trials, a factor was enthusiasm and interest. Then, as now, the riders were motivated to learn and to improvise in emergencies.

Other people who are not as qualified as the natural competitors need to work at physical conditioning or to overcome their timidity, which is preferable to brashness. A timid person can gain confidence by learning, while the brash individual is inclined to think he knows it all, and in his ignorance may blunder into disaster. The mere fact that a timid person wants to participate in a distance Ride is a step forward. As training progresses, the rider will gain confidence while his body is strengthening.

The overweight need to lose pounds; the sedentary to exercise. Swimming, tennis, golf — almost any sport — are helpful, and if a person lives in a northern climate and lacks access to a covered ring, he will have to keep in shape by whatever exercise is available, but he should not forget that riding employs muscles that are not used in other sports, and that as soon as possible he should get on a horse.

And yet, despite the emphasis on conditioning the rider like the horse, neither age nor physical handicaps prohibit a few brave people from competing. Frances Huling of Yucaipa, California, had polio as a child which left her with a partially paralyzed right leg and foot. Refusing to accept a sedentary role, Miss Huling started competing in North American Trail Ride Conference events. She rode an English cavalry saddle which was more comfortable for her than a western saddle, and shortened one stirrup for her bad leg. To mount, she got on the off side. Not only did Miss Huling ride in numerous 40-mile competitions, she finished the year 1961 by being the high-point champion of NATRC.

Another well known competitive rider, a man, has a pacemaker in his heart, while a gentleman on the eastern circuit has one leg several inches shorter than the other. And in the Rocky Mountain Conference, a man 82 years old won the Reserve Championship.

"Grandmother," I heard a child say to a grey-haired woman as the two waited on their horses by the starting line, "I hope I win a blue ribbon like the ones you've won."

These people are young and strong in heart.

Whatever shape a rider is in, he may benefit by hints from experienced distance riders, some of whom carry energy bars or packets of nuts and raisins. If they drink, it is juice or water, never carbonated beverages, and they do not overeat the night before a Ride or at breakfast. Some people can take salt tablets in hot weather; others find they make them ill. Vitamin B shots act as a booster for some riders, if a doctor can be persuaded that a person who can ride forty miles in six and a half hours needs a pep-up. The shot could be psychosomatic, too.

Another helpful hint is that in case of leg cramps after a Ride, a teaspoonful of bicarbonate of soda in a half glass of water is an effective remedy.

Clothing is important. Unlike the rider in the show ring where the emphasis is on correct apparel, the distance rider is interested in comfort. In Vermont, Virginia, and a number of other eastern Rides, the contestants sometimes wear hunt caps, breeches, and boots of the approved fashion, but costumes can be varied and of no definable style. A rider may have western boots, jeans, and a beach hat; or jeans and a T-shirt; or jodphurs and tennis shoes; although usually only the experts on Endurance Rides wear tennis shoes.

Many contestants pride themselves on their strange headgear, which is festooned with pins and mementoes from previous events. While this is entertaining, the motivating factor is that the hat provides protection from the sun; the footgear is suitable to the exigencies of the Ride; and the rest of the costume fits the purpose. High nylon socks, or better still, light silk or cotton underwear, will prevent chafing. If the weather is chilly or threatens rain, a jacket or slicker should be carried on the back of the saddle. Personally, I never go out on any kind of day without a jacket, for there are times when I return from a ride later than expected and the jacket proves more than welcome.

A small pouch which can be purchased at most sporting goods stores, and which fits on the belt, holds necessities such as aspirin, Kleenex, a hoof pick, a pen knife, salt tablets, or energy bars. The trail map furnished by the management can be folded in the pouch bag or carried in a pocket. An orange and a flashlight can be rolled into the jacket on the back of the saddle. Oranges don't squash and they ease thirst, while the flashlight is needed at night on a 100-mile Endurance event.

Needless to say, a contestant should not buy a new pair of boots a few days before the Ride, or he might develop blisters. Nor are new jeans a good idea. Old ones that have been softened by many washings are the best. Another suggestion is to wear elastic bandages around the knees outside the jeans, which some riders say prevents their knees from aching.

If dead weight has to be carried to fit the weight qualifications for divisions on Endurance Rides, the problem can be solved by using a heavier saddle or carrying a thick jacket or chaps, or by lead in pockets made for the purpose. Or a rider might emulate the military trial contestants who carried extra sets of horseshoes, rasps, and nails in pommel containers. Whatever the arrangement, dead weight is a disadvantage.

Equally important to both horse and rider are the saddle, bridle, and blanket or pad, for they affect the comfort of the rider as well as the horse. A rule to remember is not to purchase new equipment just before an event. A new, stiff saddle can rub animal and rider; a bit to which a horse is unaccustomed can irritate his mouth; and a fancy blanket can cause heat bumps on his back. The horse's shoes, the saddle, the rider's boots — indeed, all of the horse's and rider's equipment — should be tested beforehand. Well-meaning friends might suggest trying this energy pill: "It did wonders for me." Or someone else might say, "Try this saddle pad; it's the best thing on the market." So the rider buys the new pad and takes the pill, with the result that he develops a bad stomach ache and the horse gets a sore back.

However, this does not mean that a contestant should not benefit from suggestions from other riders, for the way to learn is to listen and observe. Every Ride varies, and the successful rider profits from his experiences and those of his competitors. With few exceptions, horsemen are generous about sharing their knowledge, and this is particularly true among distance riders.

The majority will say that at one time or another they have experimented with various types of saddles — the McClellan, the Steubben, the Phillips, stock saddles, custom-made models. Their reasons for doing so are varied, but not many people are familiar with the anatomy of a horse's back, which plays such a vital part in the selection of a saddle.

If a person looks at an anatomical drawing of a horse, he will see that the back consists of eighteen vertebrae of the spinal column and of the ribs. All the vertebrae are padded with muscle, but since they lie close to the surface, they must be protected from pressure. During training, the muscles and excess fat along the spine and adjoining area harden, changing the shape of the back, which means that the saddle fits differently after conditioning than it did before. Therefore, it behooves a person to buy a saddle from a reliable firm, for good saddles are made with this in mind.

The withers, insulated by muscle, comprise the first eight vertebrae, six or seven of which are usually longer than the others, and to which are attached the suspensory ligaments of the neck and various muscles of the back, shoulders, and ribs. The upper ends of the shoulder blades are topped with thick cartilage and are located on each side of the withers. The shoulder blades are not connected to the spinal column by bone, but by strong muscles that control the movements. For instance, when the horse extends his foot, the lower part of the shoulder blade comes forward and up and around the center of motion, while the upper part of the shoulder blade swings back and down.

If we are aware of this, we realize that the saddle must be placed in a position where it does not interfere with the movement of the shoulder blades. In addition, the saddle should clear the top of the withers by three fingers, and should not be so narrow that it pinches, nor so wide that it sits down on the spine.

Col. W. H. Carter wrote that, "the longer the surface over which a given amount of pressure is equally spread, the less will be the action on any given point of the other surface in contact. The under surface of the saddle should bear as nearly as possible the same relation to that part of the horse's back it is intended to occupy as a mold does to a cast, always keeping in mind that the horse's backbone should not be in contact with the saddle."

The best policy is to try out a saddle. Most shops have a sawhorse over which the saddle can be slung so that the potential customer can sit in it, but this is not as satisfactory as cinching the saddle on a live animal and riding a few miles. Perhaps a friend has a saddle similar to one that the prospective customer wants to buy, and he can borrow it.

A man should feel natural and relaxed in a saddle that fits him; he should experience no tension from the position of the stirrups or the shape of the seat. His weight should be forward, not back on the cantle where it interferes with the horse's stride.

In English and in some western saddles, according to Jean Saint-Fort Paillard, noted French equestrian, "The rider should sit as far forward in the saddle as possible on the fatty part of his buttocks, with his weight evenly distributed."

The position of the buttocks is important, because it determines the position of the torso and of the legs.

Until recently, eastern and European contestants rode flat saddles, and westerners rode stock saddles, but this has changed. In the New Jersey, Florida, and other eastern Rides, contestants use both types of saddles, while the Steubben (a flat saddle made in Germany) has become popular with competitors in the West and Midwest.

The first question a prospective purchaser should ask himself is, what do I want the saddle for? Saddles are as varied as automobiles, the west-

SADDLE RIGGING

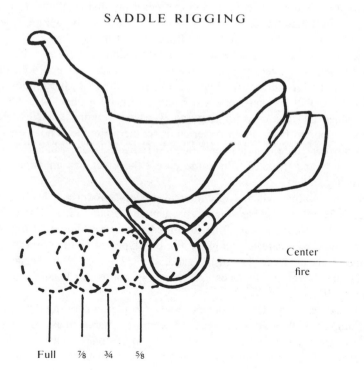

Center

fire

Full   ⅞   ¾   ⅝

ern models being styled on different trees for bulldogging, cutting, ranch work, calf-roping, and pleasure. In a roping saddle, the stirrups have no forward swing, since they are designed for quick dismounting, while the California equitation type, fine in the show ring, would not do for competitive riding because it is made for a person who sits back against the cantle.

The rigging also differs. There is the ¾, the ⅝, the full rigging, and the center fire. The majority of western saddles are doublerigged with a cinch and flank strap (fillet), the purpose of the latter being to hold the saddle down when roping or going down a steep hill. Calf ropers prefer the full, or ⅞, rigging, which is set forward. The center fire, which was once popular, is seldom seen today. Perhaps the most widely used is the ¾, which appears to be the favorite rigging for distance riding. The cinch is less apt to gall a horse, and if the saddle needs to be held in place, a breast collar can be used.

Indeed, so popular has distance riding become that a number of companies modify saddles on request, and one company manufactures a saddle designed by Sharon Saare of the Appaloosa Horse Club, with a ¾ rigging, a minimum of skirt, and a modified swell with no horn.

The stirrups on the saddle are already cushioned. As any distance rider knows, tape over sponge or foam rubber strips wrapped with tape provide a pad for the foot that can be a help on the long, hard miles.

No saddle will last long unless it is made of good leather. The best is bark-tanned and comes from England, Germany, or the United States. Leather imported from South America or southern Europe is not as good, but is a better grade than leather tanned in India or Japan, which is apt to crack, curl, and discolor. In some cases, the latter has an unpleasant odor if it gets wet.

Chrome-tanning, which is a chemical process, produces a leather that is not as flexible as the bark-tanned product and is more difficult to clean. Since leather does not have to be identified as to where it came from, the buyer should take care to recognize the two types of tanning and to find out the origin of the leather in the saddle he is buying. The cheaper the saddle, the better the chances are that it is poorly made and that the leather will not last.

Flat saddles vary, too, being designed for pleasure riding, dressage, and jumping with a forward seat. The most reliable trees, reinforced with steel, are manufactured in England and in Germany. Distance riders who use an English saddle agree with those equestrians who say that the more leather there is between the leg and the horse, the less feel the rider has for the horse. Knee rolls are a matter of preference for the individual rider.

Usually there is at least one McClellan, and occasionally a Phillips, on a Ride, these being U.S. military models that are no longer made, and for that reason, difficult to find. The 1936 Phillips officers' saddle has an 18½-inch seat and was intended for cross-country work. Dr. Richard Barsaleau rode a Phillips for 26 years until, as he said, it fell to pieces. I have one, and although it is a trifle large, it is comfortable and does not sore a horse's back. Unlike some earlier military models, it does not have long bars, which exerted pressure on the loin area.

The 1928 McClellan, which was the last model made, has a split tree and was designed to fit all kinds of horses except those with broad backs and low withers, which is the reason many people do not like it. Personally, I find it uncomfortable, although it is well-made and durable and weighs very little.

Any saddle, if bought second-hand, should have a sound tree and be in good condition, for no saddle with a broken tree can be ridden, and leather cannot be restored to what it was originally, particularly if it is cracked or flaked. Neatsfoot oil might seem to make it pliable, but the appearance is deceiving. While oil can darken leather, it is not advisable to continue using it.

Water, as everyone knows, is damaging, and when saddle soaping, the water should be carefully rationed. If a saddle is scabbed with mud, it is better to let it dry and scrape it off than to wash it with water. A preparation with a lanolin base is recommended by experts for keeping leather in good condition.

Whatever is used — saltless tallow, soap, or oil — hours of rubbing go into the care of tack. Mechanical walkers have been invented to make it easier to cool horses, but so far no one has invented a substitute for cleaning leather. How often my dishes have been left in the sink while I sat on the steps of the tack room soaping a dismembered bridle! And when I do the laundry, clothes are apt to come out tufted with horse's hair, a residue of blankets that were a previous wash.

Girths are another item to be considered. They can be of leather, elastic webbing, or mohair, and can be padded with sheepskin or the new synthetics, such as Equi-Fleece. Blankets are made of synthetics also, and many people use them because they protect the horse's back. A disadvantage is that they retain the heat, increasing the possibility of heat

SADDLE INJURIES

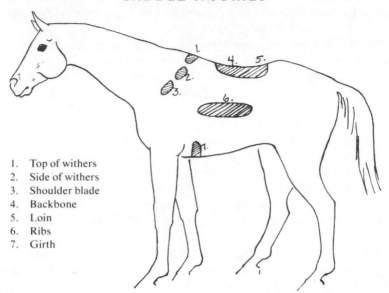

1. Top of withers
2. Side of withers
3. Shoulder blade
4. Backbone
5. Loin
6. Ribs
7. Girth

bumps. I also found that some synthetic pads slip and bunch beneath the saddle, particularly beneath a flat saddle, but if the pads are lined with linen or other similar material, the problem is solved. The fact that synthetics come in brilliant colors as well as white appeals to many people. On one Ride, a brunette had a scarlet padded breast collar, cinch, and fleece blanket. To complete the color scheme, she wore a scarlet shirt. Occasionally contestants such as this girl experience a feeling of frustration because of the indifference of other competitors to attire, but after they have ridden a number of Rides, they, too, concentrate on comfort rather than eye appeal.

In one Army Endurance trial, the riders used wool blankets next to the horse, with an O.D. issue blanket on top. Another wool blanket, the genuine Navajo, has long been a favorite, but unfortunately Navajos are expensive and hard to find, and the imitations are not as thick or as tightly woven. Hair pads are also used by many contestants, the type similar to those favored by outfitters for their pack horses.

Many experienced distance riders feel that the blanket and/or the pads are vitally important. Some people who ride English saddles use a single, light pad but they risk injury to the horse's back. The more protection the horse has the better, which does not mean piling on blankets and pads indiscriminately, but rather experimenting until the horse is comfortable after a long ride and does not flinch when hands are pressed along the spine. Indeed, one of the tests veterinarians give for soundness is putting pressure on the horse's back.

Blankets, cinches, and breast collar covers should be dried out after use and cleaned frequently, for the sweat and dirt that accumulates can cause sores.

Now for that small but important item of equipment, the bit, which should be any kind in which the horse is comfortable and to which he is accustomed. A contestant may use a snaffle and a stock saddle or a hackamore and a flat saddle. The type of bit does not need to correspond to the remainder of the outfit. Bits with long shanks, high ports that rub the roof of the mouth, and twisted wire snaffles are severe. Gag bits should never be used. Severe bits, unless employed by an expert, can cut the horse's mouth and cause him to be fractious. Indeed, hard-mouthed horses are more apt to bolt than horses with good mouths and easy bits. A medium shank, low port, and thick mouthpiece, such as there are in hollow mouth curbs, are easy on a horse's mouth.

A rider should make sure the bit fits his horse; that it isn't too wide or too narrow, which will cause it to pinch. Contrary to what some people might imagine, horses' mouths are not the same size, which means that in the case of the snaffle, it should be adjusted so that there is one wrinkle in the corner of the mouth, while a curb should be fit up in the corner of the mouth with no wrinkles. If it is too low, it will knock against the front teeth.

The bosal hackamores are increasing in popularity, and some of the most proficient Endurance riders prefer them. On several Rides I have also seen horses ridden with halters.

Much, of course, depends on the rider's hands, which should be sensitive enough to maintain control and at the same time help the horse. The experienced rider keeps a light contact with the horse's mouth while giving the animal freedom of his head.

Seldom do we find standing or running martingales on distance rides. I have seen a few, and of the two types the running martingale is preferred by the riders who use them. The objection to martingales is that they do not allow the horse the freedom of his head that is necessary while traveling over rough ground for many miles. If the horse is well trained for the purpose, he should not need an artificial aid.

11. The Horse Goes Touring

A BYSTANDER, seeing Voodoo walk into the trailer, observed, "That's worth five hundred dollars right there."

We were loading horses at night. During the day, the Arizona desert bakes in the sun, so we had decided to travel after dark when it was cool. The moon silver-plated the dry arroyos and cactus; shadows blackened the stables and riding ring. Our convoy consisted of three horse vans, which were owned by a friend who had offered a space for Voodoo as a courtesy. If I'd had to spend hours fighting to load the mare, I might not have been able to take her north, since I could not hold up the convoy. This was one of many experiences that convinced me how important it is for a horse to load.

In the case of distance horses, it is a necessity, for they are hauled hundreds of miles to Rides and are often trailered shorter distances several times a week for training.

To a novice, loading a mature, untrained horse into a trailer might seem easy, but this is a gross misconception. Strong men have been tempted to throw themselves on the ground and weep after hours of frustrating work to load a horse, and this includes trainers and experienced equestrians who boast they can load any horse in any kind of vehicle.

If the novice seeks information about loading, he will receive a variety of answers; horsemen seldom agree, and each one is sure his way is the only way. However, no one will dispute the fact that the gentlest horse can turn into a balky beast when he approaches a trailer. If he snorts, rears, and rolls his eyes, he is probably frightened; if he braces himself and refuses to budge, he is probably stubborn. Why he reacts the way he does is important, for the stubborn horse should be dealt with differently from the animal that is afraid.

The Palomino I once had was stubborn. From his previous owner I learned he had not been abused or frightened in a trailer; he simply did not want to get in one. The first method I employed is recommended by numerous trainers. Backing the trailer into the corral, I blocked the wheels and set a pail of grain on the floor inside. The Palomino put his front feet on the edge of the trailer and with his hind feet braced behind him as far as they would go, stretched his neck until he could reach the bucket. This performance was repeated for a number of times; then I moved the bucket further into the trailer. The Palomino refused to venture after it — he'd starve first. At this point, I wished he would starve, but, instead, I tried another solution to the problem. With the help of a friend, we put a rope behind the Palomino and tried to boost him in, whereupon he stuck out his lower lip and stood like a rock.

A bowlegged old jockey told me once, "Never let a horse know he's bigger than you are."

This was one time the horse knew it. All right; we'd try another well-known trick. We loaded an obedient old plug into the adjoining stall in the trailer, hoping the Palomino would benefit from the example. See, Old Pal got in; why don't you?

We rattled the grain pail; we waved our hats in the rear of the cream-colored rump. No luck. My patience began to fray. It was hot and I was sweating. My husband, who had helped during the first stage, left for the house, saying, "Why don't you shoot him?"

I was tempted to follow the advice, but restrained my anger. If I lost my temper, I might as well give up. The horse would only become more uncooperative and I would end up in an hysterical heap on the ground.

Patience. Patience. Whenever a horse gets away with not going into a trailer, he becomes more difficult to work with in the future. In *Western Horseman* I had read of a man who, when loading untrained horses, fitted them with opaque goggles so that, blind to their surroundings and dependent on the person leading them, they followed their handler into the trailer without protest.

But somehow I didn't think that would work with the Palomino.

Another thing occurred to me. Some trailers had ramps; ours did not, which meant that the horse had to step up. Often this will cause problems, for horses do not like routine to be varied.

A whip to flick the Palomino on the hocks? This was rejected, although many trainers employ the whip successfully. When I had tried it, or had seen trainers try it, the horse had kicked and I did not want a horse who kicked every time he was loaded.

In the end, we got tough — not angry-tough, but firm — as one does with a spoilt child. My friend tied the Palomino by a long rope to a ring by the feed box, and then, with a rope around the Palomino's haunches, a waving hat and shouts, forced the horse inside. When the door was shut and the butt strap fastened, the Palomino was allowed to stand for a while eating grain and hay. Then he was unloaded and the process repeated.

After this, the Palomino did not object to being loaded, although I had reservations about tying the horse to a ring, which could have been hazardous. The horse could have thrown up his head and cut himself against the roof or side of the trailer.

In the case of a frightened horse, the important thing is to get him to relax and to acquire confidence in the person trying to load him. To hurry or rush matters is fatal. Infinite patience is required. Lead the horse to the trailer, stop and give him some grain and pet him. Then gradually coax him into the trailer, a little way at a time; give him more grain and talk to him. If he tries to back out, prevent him if possible. A lead shank on a chain is a help in this regard, but don't let the horse fight. If he becomes panicky, allow him to back out, then try to restore his confidence and ease him gradually into the trailer again.

The most satisfactory solution to teaching horses to load is to train them when they are young. A walk-through trailer — that is, a trailer that has an escape door large enough for an animal or man — is ideal. The foal can be led up the ramp into the trailer and out the door. In addition, these trailers have ceilings high enough so that there is no danger of a foal cracking his head if he throws it up in sudden fright. After the foal has been led through the trailer a number of times, he can be fastened in and given grain and hay. Eventually he can be taken for a short ride.

Many horses have been frightened by being banged around by poor drivers who jam on the brakes suddenly and wheel around curves like a Grand Prix racer. To see how this feels, the driver should ride in the trailer himself, an experience that might cause him to be more responsible on the road in the future.

Sometimes it is a good idea to use shipping boots or leg wraps to protect a horse's legs. Shipping boots can be purchased at most tack shops, as can leg wraps, although if the latter are used, they should be put on correctly — not too tight, limiting circulation, or too lose, so as to come undone.

When Voodoo was loaded, she expressed her dislike of being confined in a small space by kicking. To keep her from splintering the door, I had to have it lined with metal. One day when Voodoo was kicking more than usual, I noticed that the trailer window was so smudged that the mare couldn't see out. After I'd cleaned the plexiglass, Voodoo's kicks became less frequent. If she could keep one wicked eye glued to the window, she felt secure, or as secure as she ever would in a small space.

Mazda, on the other hand, has never shown the slightest fear of a trailer except for one or two times when he was grazing in a mountain meadow and did not want to leave the delectable grass. I did not train Mazda to load, but whoever did, I am sure he had no difficulty if he rattled an oat bucket or proffered an orange.

Horses distrust trailers for many reasons: they have been hauled for too long a time without unloading and become trailer sour, or they have been left unblanketed in cold weather or allowed to smother in the heat. Or the trailer was too small and they were cramped; or the floor was slippery, so they had trouble keeping their footing on rough roads. Again, the distance rider might remember that a horse is no different from a person. He does not want to repeat an unpleasant experience.

Horses can be hauled in stock trucks, in one- or two-horse trailers, or in vans as long and elaborate as Pullman cars. Which type a person buys depends on his individual needs and preferences. Nearly all commercially manufactured vehicles are a good investment, but care should be taken if a person buys a home-made model.

Some people advocate unloading every three and one-half to four hours; five hours might be permissible on a long haul. The horse can be led around and allowed to graze. There are usually turn-outs and rest areas which can be utilized for this purpose. However, if a horse is difficult to load, it might be advisable to continue to the night stop.

Where to stay at night? Fairgrounds have stalls, but sometimes they must be cleaned and disinfected. Or riding and hunt clubs might have accommodations.

In Tuscaloosa, Alabama, one evening, we pulled into a motel to find out where we could keep a horse for the night. I got out to look through the telephone book and to talk to the desk clerk. The yellow pages are invaluable; the sheriff, veterinarians, and feed and grain stores listed in the directory are sources of information. As it turned out, we did not have to inquire. An elderly gentleman, hearing me speak to the desk clerk, approached courteously.

"Ma'am, I heard you ask where you could keep a horse tonight. I can help you. We have a hunt club at the edge of town. If you'll follow me, I'll lead you out."

This was true southern hospitality. It is amazing how often a person encounters helpful people when he is hauling horses.

In an emergency, a horse can be left in the trailer all night. We did this once with Flower Child at a motel in Tennessee. We parked the trailer directly outside the window and all went well until a man came by and slapped Flower Child on the rump. At the resulting fracas, Tex leapt from the bathtub, wrapped herself in a towel, and dashed out to quiet a wild-eyed animal. A horse can also stand tied outside the trailer all night in a camping area. Personally we like to stay close to our horses, and unless we find good stalls at a fairground or a hunt club similar to the one in Alabama, we prefer sleeping bags. One can always wash the following night.

Another lesson we learned was to stop early. It is difficult to locate fairgrounds in the dark, and the veterinary clinics and feed stores ordinarily close in late afternoon.

One competitive rider whom I know, a grandmother with grey hair, pulls off to the side of the road at night to sleep in her pickup truck. When her horse, an experienced campaigner, thinks she's slept long enough, he bangs on the trailer until she wakes. Unfortunately, what the Appaloosa considers a full night's rest is only a few hours.

Anyone who has hauled horses has experienced mechanical failures and flat tires, usually on the loneliest stretch of road, late at night, in a storm, miles from a service station. A mechanically inclined man strong enough to change a tire on a van can deal with the situation, but less fortunate individuals might have trouble. Distance riders are more ingenious than the average person; they have to be. But not all of them know a carburetor from a fuel pump, nor can they jack up a van. Therefore, it behooves a distance rider, before starting on a trip, to check his trailer as well as his car. Is the hitch in good shape? Are the electrical connections working so that the signal lights and brakes respond as they should? Is the feed box clean? Has the rubber floor mat been taken out and the boards checked to see if they are sound? Tires? Door locks? When hooking a trailer to a car or truck, a person should make sure that the cup on the trailer fits over the ball on the car and that the lock is in place; also that the safety chains are fastened and the electric connection plugged in.

Most station wagons and cars need air shocks to haul a trailer. These not only stabilize the car, but lift it when air pressure is put in, so that the hitch fits on the ball. Equally important is to be sure that the vehicle is large enough to pull a trailer. A four- or six-cylinder compact auto might save on gasoline, but it does not have the power to haul a trailer on the highway, to say nothing of pulling one up the Adirondacks or over a pass in the Rockies. Even an eight-cylinder car can encounter difficulties on a two-lane road that zigzags 5000 feet in ten miles. How unnerving it is to feel the engine jerk and slow on a grade that drops to a rock-strewn canyon, no guide rail and no place to pull out! We usually try to maintain a speed of 25 to 30 miles an hour on a steep road, which is not always possible if a truck is grinding at fifteen miles an hour in low gear just ahead. Then the only thing to do is to stop at the nearest wide place and wait until the truck has reached the summit.

In our cross-country travels with horses, we have encountered floods, near-tornadoes, mud, electrical storms, and heat that caused the engines to vapor-lock, but the most frightening experience is to feel the trailer skid on ice — to see it swing from side to side, and to know that if it jackknifes it will go off the road or be smashed by an oncoming car. Whatever the driver does, he must not jam on his brakes; he can only guide the car to the best of his ability and hope the good Lord is watching over him, which is more likely if he has a four-wheel drive.

Unless there is an emergency, we do not haul horses in the winter on bad roads, and then we have heavy-duty, studded tires and chains for the trailer, in case they are needed.

We also travel main highways, the Interstates when possible. Side roads might tempt by less mileage, but time can be lost by curves, chuckholes, and steep grades. When we don't know the road, we trace our route on a map which we keep in the glove compartment with health and vaccination certificates for the horses, registration papers, and brand inspection permits, which are mandatory in western states.

In the tack room in the trailer are saddles, blankets, bridles, halters and lead ropes, buckets, grain and hay, and the tack box that is crammed with grooming equipment, fly spray, tincture of violet, and other remedies. One of the first things that a distance rider learns is that traveling with a horse is like traveling with a circus. Indeed, we have been taken for a circus when driving in convoy with three horse vans.

In a small western town, a drunk staggered up to peer owlishly at the lead van, whose windows and door were closed in the cold morning air.

"What you got in there?"

"Trained llamas," my husband said.

"Oh." Satisfied, the drunk staggered off.

As a matter of courtesy, the contestant should arrive at the Ride area in plenty of time to unload and sign in before the veterinary inspection. Nothing annoys the management or the judges more than a contestant who appears after the judges have finished the preliminary check and are snatching a quick bite to eat before the briefing. The check-in time is noted on the entry blank, so that except for an emergency there is no excuse for being late.

If the Ride is in a National Forest or an isolated area, the rider should find out beforehand where to turn off the highway. Usually the route is marked by the Ride management, but a map might be helpful if a marker were torn down or poorly placed.

As soon as the contestant arrives at his destination, he should go to the Secretary for directions about where to put his horse and where to stay himself. He should not, without permission, shove his rig into the most desirable place in the camp, which might be reserved for judging or for social activities. Nor should he park his trailer too close to another contestant; and if he is late, he should accept whatever space is available with good grace, which could mean he sleeps on cactus or is besieged by mosquitoes from a nearby swamp, or is forced to put his blankets on a downhill slope, so that if it rains he becomes submerged.

A camper or camper insert keeps the rider immune from the weather and has an additional advantage that he can make himself a cup of coffee before the cook is astir. The back of a good-sized station wagon can also be a comfortable bed, and I have seen people sleep in horse trailers, in all manner of tents, and beneath stock trucks. How and where a rider stays depends to a large extent on the part of the country where he is competing. In the West, a sleeping bag is acceptable; in Virginia, breakfast can be served in bed at The Homestead.

Motels and lodges, some elaborate and some simple, are increasingly available for accommodations, and these are most satisfactory if they are not too far from the Ride area. A knowledgeable contestant never leaves his horse unattended unless the animal is in a good stall where a night watchman makes the rounds, or if the horse is tied to the trailer, unless he has made arrangements with a reliable friend to care for his animal.

The Secretary will give the rider his number, a map, and directions about the briefing and check-in. Then the horse can be unloaded, fed, watered, and groomed. Usually there is a creek nearby, or a spigot or water truck. Old friends are greeted and new ones introduced. In the West, informality is the rule and people are on a first-name basis; in the East it is more difficult to get acquainted. However, East or West, everyone is united by a common bond of interest in the horses and in each other. There are the Endurance Rides where the pros know the tricks of the trade and the contest can be tough, particularly if money is awarded as a prize. Everyone recognizes these top performers and inspects them with interest — the horse as lean and bony as a whippet; his rider. Heroes in the world of distance riding. Then there are the people who have ridden but never placed highly because they were not sufficiently competitive, or did not have an adequate horse or one that was conditioned. There are those who hope to win, or who ride for pleasure or the challenge. There are the beginners who have high hopes; those who are tense and fearful; the too-confident.

Some will make it, some will not. Fundamentally, this does not matter; what does is that, for the moment, the urbanized universe is forgotten in the contest of men and horses on the trail.

12. Rides: From Florida's Sands to the Sierras

BEFORE a person competes, he should determine the number of Rides he intends to enter. Some people will sign up for only one Ride; others will go to as many as possible, depending on whether or not they are hoping to win a trophy, such as the President's Cup awarded to the rider who gathers the most points on NATRC Rides, or the Eastern United States 100-Mile Challenge Trophy awarded by the Florida Horsemen's Association to the rider who has accumulated the most points in three 100-mile Rides during the year. The Rides sanctioned for this last trophy are the Florida, Virginia, New Jersey, New York, Maine, Vermont and North Carolina Rides.

All Rides appreciate receiving entries as soon as possible. For the Tevis, some riders enter for the following year shortly after the Ride of that summer is finished; the Florida Ride insists on entries by January 10 for the Ride which is held in mid-March; the Old Dominion 100-Mile Endurance Ride at Leesburg, Virginia, requests entries a month previous to the event. On the other hand, some Rides accept entries up to the day before. If a competitor does not make sure of the entry deadline, he might arrive for an event only to discover that the list is closed.

In the United States, there are more than 500 Distance Rides, and additional ones are being listed every year. Canada has Rides; so do England, Germany, and Australia. As noted above, the rules, judging, and terrain vary in each area.

What are the similarities and the differences? It might be helpful to examine the organizations that sponsor the Rides.

The largest, and one of the best-organized associations, is the North American Trail Ride Conference — the NATRC — based in California. Since it was established in 1961, it has encouraged the care and breeding of horses, their training and conditioning, and good horsemanship. In particular, the Conference has furthered pulse, temperature, and respiration as criteria of conditioning.

For a year I was on the board of the NATRC and attended a meeting one autumn at Mount Diablo in Concord, not far from San Francisco. Mount Diablo has a clubhouse and paddocks among the oak trees, and could be said to be the birthplace of NATRC, for one of the first Rides was held on the mountain and along the coastal range, and there is still an annual Mount Diablo Competitive event. If I remember correctly, there were about 75 NATRC members at the clubhouse from California, Washington, Montana, and Arizona. After an open meeting, a closed session was held by the board in a small room lit by an unshaded bulb among stacked boxes and other excess paraphernalia. The discussion was heated and lasted until midnight.

"Should we allow leading?"

"What about pads?"

I looked at the men around the table — veterinarians and businessmen, none of whom were paid for their time, and who were yet as concerned about these problems as they would have been about a severe colic or a merger. Why?

The veterinarians might be explained. One present was engaged in research at Davis, an agricultural branch of the University of California. Any good veterinarian is interested in the effects of stress on horses, and distance Rides can tell them more about that subject than a laboratory experiment. As for the businessmen, a number had children with whom they enjoyed riding as a family hobby. The remaining two members of the board simply liked horses and horse activities.

They had their gripes, however. One member protested, "I'm spending too much time on this!"

Another exclaimed, "Hell, we all spend too much time on it, but we've got to get it off the ground!"

They were not content to relax with the few Rides that already belonged to the Conference; their goal was to expand until they had Rides all over the United States. They would be the biggest and the best. Such is the California creed, where world championships multiply among the oak trees and freeways. Yet these NATRC members did not promote a hard sell. They were purely nonprofit and growth to them meant that many more horses taken care of and that many more people learning to become good riders. They were not trying to reach the professionals, but the average person with an average horse. Who could help respecting such an attitude?

It was inevitable that once the idea had been planted and nurtured by such dedicated people, it would sprout in the genial atmosphere of the Pacific coast. Of California's 21 million inhabitants, vast numbers own one or more horses which they keep in backyard lots. They have the leisure and the money to go to Rides. In addition, they have a climate that permits year-round outdoor activity, and as varied terrain as anywhere in the nation.

Since my time on the Board, the NATRC has fulfilled its potential. The Board no longer meets in storerooms, but in more luxurious surroundings in Colorado and Arizona, as well as in California, and shortly they will be meeting in the Midwest and in the East, for the Association has 52 Rides in most states of the Union and in Canada.

On a recent visit to California, I stopped by to visit Joan Throgmorton, who has been the secretary of the NATRC during its amazing period of growth. The Throgmortons live on a small ranch outside of Gilroy, where Dr. B. C. Throgmorton has a practice. One of the most knowledgeable veterinarian judges, Dr. Throgmorton has also ridden in Rides and has written widely on pulse and respiration.

The white farmhouse is backed by a large, old-fashioned barn, surrounded by fields where horses graze. The Throgmortons are interested in breeding distance horses, which does not mean registered animals, but horses with the conformation, stamina, and heart to compete on the trails. Joan Throgmorton has short, curly hair, a friendly manner, and immense vitality, which she needs for housekeeping, ranch chores, competing as a high-point contestant in the NATRC Rides, and serving as the unpaid secretary of the Conference. Leading me into a back room, Joan showed me files crammed with membership cards, lists of sanctioned Rides, Rides requesting sanction, letters of inquiry, and business communications. From a cupboard, she selected colored sheets and pamphlets, explaining that they were the *NATRC Management Manual;* the *Rider's Manual;* an *Introduction to Competitive Trail Riding;* a rule book; information sheets such as the one to all ride managers on the subject of time and mileage on Rides; the sheet that is sent to Rides when they have been approved for NATRC membership; the Ride Report Sheet which must be filled out and sent to NATRC Headquarters on completion of a Ride; the NATRC horsemanship scorecard; the official scorecard; directions to Ride stewards; more directions to Ride managers about insurance; insurance forms; directions for judges' secretaries and recorders; pulse and respiration forms to be used by the Rides; lists of approved judges; forms for confidential reports from the Ride stewards; the *Newsletter* forwarded to members each month.

When I had the opportunity to read the information supplied me, I saw that the Rides Manual contains detailed instructions about caring for the horse in the stall and when tied outside (e.g., fasten the water bucket securely, so the horse can't kick it over); how to present the horse to the judges (lead from the left side of the horse and hold the upper end of the leadline in the right hand); equipment (carry a pocket comb to get cholla cactus off the horse's legs in Arizona); how to mount; how to time oneself (count riding time, subtract lunch stop and PR stops); how to ride on a trail (in general, keep horse at a walk when climbing or going downhill); post-ride inspection.

The other manuals and instruction sheets are as informative as detailed, so that every question that might be asked is answered.

NATRC has family and individual memberships. In addition, each Ride pays so much per rider to cover the expenses of material mailed to them, such as judges' and P and R sheets. Meals and accommodations are in addition to the entry fee.

A Class C Ride, newly instituted, is a three-day event. A Class A Ride is two days, thirty to forty miles each day of approximately 6½ to 7 hours of riding time. The riding time is similar in the Class C Ride, and also the Class B Ride, which is a one-day Ride. Normally, riding speed for open riders is 3.8 to 4.8 miles per hour.

Judging is 40 percent on soundness, which includes heat and swelling in the tendons and joints, lameness, muscle soreness, and saddle and cinch sores; 40 percent on condition, which includes pulse and respiration, signs of fatigue, and ability to continue; manners, 15 percent. Way of going, 5 percent, subtracting for any abnormal action or gait that interferes with the horse's action.

Lay judges, stewards, and veterinary judges are employed on NATRC Rides.

As for the differences between NATRC Rides and some other associations, the NATRC allows manmade obstacles on the trail, no pads are allowed, leading is restricted, and no care of the horse is permitted at night.

Rules are changed periodically and can be drastically altered if a different type of judging is adopted. For this reason, the current rules of all associations and Rides should be studied before competing.

The *Newsletter* that is mailed to members monthly contains information on the Rides that are sponsored by NATRC from Georgia to Missouri to California. The Skull Mesa Ride, which is usually held in April in Arizona, is one of these events. The campsite is among trees on Rancho Mañana, and the trail climbs up the famous mesa for which the Ride is named, through cliffs and canyons. On the slopes, cactus squats among the boulders; in the canyons cottonwoods cluster along trickles of water. This Ride, with its steep climbs, can be exciting in inclement weather.

Another NATRC Ride is at Gilroy Hot Springs, put on by the San Martin Horsemen, in May. Camp is along Cayote Creek, which at this time of year is filled with water, and not, as so many California stream beds are later in the year, dried to sand bars and pebbles. Gilroy is what a person might imagine a California Ride would be — a trail that winds through oak trees and along the crest of coastal hills blurred by fog in the early morning, and warmed by the sun later in the day. One of the most popular Rides, Gilroy has as many as 160 contestants, but so efficient have the San Martin Horsemen become that they manage outdoor barbecues and pancakes and sausages for breakfast, for which a reasonable charge is made.

The only difficulty an NATRC member might have, reading the list of coming Rides for the year, might be which event to enter — the Ride at the Air Force Academy at Colorado Springs in May; Griffith Park in Los Angeles in March; the Robbers Route Ride in Oklahoma in August; the Cotton Picking Trail Ride in Georgia in September; or the Graves Mountain Lodge Ride in Virginia, also in September. Distance is, of course, the deciding factor, which is the reason the NATRC is encouraging area conferences and trophies.

NATRC Rides are friendly gatherings — informal and brightened by practical jokes.

"We're getting too big," a Board member told me not long ago. "We need a paid secretary."

This is inevitable, in an organization dedicated to growth. No group can expect a volunteer to devote endless hours to office work, but the question arises, will the NATRC retain its attitude toward competitive trail riding as an amateur sport? Some time in the future, new officials will replace the dedicated people who established the Conference. Will growth which was promoted for the purpose of good horsemanship destroy that amateur attitude?

This is a problem facing all organizations, in particular the Endurance

Ride people in the West. So far NATRC, the Eastern Competitive Trail Ride Association, the Rocky Mountain Conference, and a number of others have withstood the pressures.

The Eastern Competitive Trail Ride Association, which was founded in 1961, lists 27 Rides, among them the best-known in the East. Like the NATRC, they have memberships. Their purpose, in addition to encouraging good horsemanship, is to promote the growth of competitive trail riding, and to provide standard rules and regulations, which is an aim shared by the other organizations. No monetary awards are allowed. Unlike the NATRC and the Rocky Mountain Conference, the ECTRA sponsors Endurance Rides. A four-year-old horse may be ridden in a Competitive Ride, while five is the age required for Endurance events. The average speed for riding time is five to six and a half miles per hour for four to seven hours, depending on the terrain. Horses must share equal accommodations; that is, they must all be tied or all stabled. No care of horses is allowed at night by the riders, and a one-hour recovery check is mandatory after the finish.

Lists of approved veterinarians and lay judges are furnished the member Rides. The ECTRA also has horsemanship judges.

Judging is 100 percent on condition, with points deducted for time over or under the maximum and minimum time limit, which is a universal rule on Competitive Rides.

The 100 percent is divided thus: 25 points for the legs — lameness and injury; 25 for pulse, respiration, dehydration, and mucous membranes; 20 points for fatigue; 15 for tack area; 10 points for attitude. Customarily the horseman judge marks tack, attitude, and fatigue, while the veterinarian checks other aspects of conditioning.

An ECTRA-sponsored Ride, the oldest in the United States (1936), is the 100-Mile in Three Days Ride held in late August in South Woodstock, Vermont. The Green Mountain Horse Association which puts on the Ride built its own stables and facilities. This is a well-organized Ride in country that resembles a Grandma Moses painting, and one of the most pleasant aspects is the pride of the community in an event which has become a New England tradition. Also an ECTRA member is the Old Dominion 100-Mile Endurance Ride held at Leesburg, Virginia, in hunt country once fought over by Union and Confederate armies. The check-in is held on the lawn before a mansion with ante-bellum columns. In 1974, when the first Ride was held, the trail followed a circular route beginning and ending at Morven Park. Eighty percent of the route — to be ridden in 24 hours — was graveled and dirt road on the level, or on gentle slopes. Unique among Endurance Rides, the Old Dominion gives a cavalry trophy for which the rider, as well as the horse, is taken into consideration. A distance riding team, the officials feel, is "only as disciplined, self-reliant and skilled as the rider-trainer. The characteristics of the good distance rider are a knowledge of caring for the athletic horse and the self-discipline to protect his horse." Perhaps other Endurance Rides will follow the example of the Old Dominion and give a similar trophy. Yet a third member of ECTRA is the Florida three-day, 100-mile Ride, sponsored by the Florida Horsemen's Association. This Ride, which takes place in March, follows trails through the Ocala National Forest. Due to the location at sea level in a semitropical climate, the Florida Ride presents a contrast to the other Rides. Deep sand that impedes the horses' going and scrub that shuts off the breeze on a hot day can present problems. There are no climbs, however, as the country is flat. Because of the sand, it is recommended that horses be shod with smooth plates. No care of the horse is allowed at night, and the contestant must take time off from his riding time for the lunch stop. Both lay and veterinarian judges are employed on this Ride. One of the older Rides in the East, the Florida 100-mile is well organized, issues numerous well-written pamphlets, and is beneficial for contestants who have ridden in the North or West in higher elevations and need the experience of competing with their horses at sea level in a humid climate.

The Rocky Mountain Conference, which is a small organization not particularly concerned with growth, has member Rides in Wyoming, Montana, and Idaho. The purpose of the organization is "to promote good horsemanship, which we define as the ability to condition and keep a horse sound for distance riding. . . . The emphasis is on what a horse can do, not how he is bred or his conformation."

The population in this area is too sparse and distances too great to attract large numbers of riders. In addition, many of the contestants are ranchers who have limited incomes and who must take time off from haying to compete. To them, riding is not a hobby, but part of the daily chores. A Trail Ride provides the opportunity to win a trophy and to learn about horses. Equally important is chatting around a campfire or in a camper with friends. The trails are spectacular and may lead across a shale slide on the Continental Divide, or through forests of ponderosa pine tangled with ferns and wild roses where elk and bear spook the horses. Rocky Mountain Rides "are not as rigorous as Endurance Rides, which are races, or as easy as some Competitive Rides; they cover a distance and type of terrain that tests both horse and rider without undue stress.''

Care of horses, is allowed at night because of the sharp temperature changes in the mountains; leading is permitted except during the last two miles; and pads are allowed.

Judging is 40 percent on condition; 40 percent on soundness; and 10 percent on manners. Lay and veterinary judges are used on most Rides. A high-point trophy, the Rocky Mountain Cup, is awarded annually; also, specially designed buckles are awarded to riders who complete three out of four Rides. Entry fees are lower than in the East, or on the West Coast; so, too, is the price of meals. Lunch is furnished free to competitors and helpers on the trail, while at the Bitterroot Trail Ride, an awards dinner is free to everyone.

There is also an Upper Midwest Endurance Ride Association, as well as associations sponsoring Competitive Rides in the area, while Canada has an association that oversees the growing number of Rides in that country.

In addition, the Appaloosa Horse Club and the International Arabian Horse Association, while not strictly Ride organizations, have done invaluable work to encourage distance riding. They issue informative pamphlets, support research and clinics, and award trophies. The Appaloosa Horse Club has a distance riding chairman and gives a medallion to eligible horses competing a specified number of miles within a calendar year.

The American Endurance Ride Conference (AERC), headquartered at Auburn, California, sponsors so many Rides that the organization has divided the country into areas, which include the West, Pacific Northwest, Southwest, Mountain West, Midwest, and Southeast. This organization, which issues excellent pamphlets and an Endurance New Year Book, has a board of directors, region directors, and a board of advisors, which includes many well-known veterinary judges and Endurance riders. The AERC publishes a list of the top ten riders and horses in each area, the horses who have completed 1000 miles in Endurance competition, and awards a trophy to the high-point rider among the leading 25 riders and horses in the American Endurance Ride Conference. Among the AERC Rides is the Castle Rock Challenge Ride, a 50-mile loop from ''ocean to ocean, through coastal redwoods.'' Other Rides are the famous Diamond 100-Miler at Red Bluff, California, the Palisades Ride in the Midwest, the Missouri 50-Mile Ride, and a number in the Southeast.

Rules are similar to those of most Endurance Rides. Horses must be five years of age and must be shod.   Awards are given to the first rider in and to the best-conditioned horse among the top ten.

While these organizations have done much to standardize rules and encourage well-managed Rides, they suffer a serious handicap in that not all maintain a permanent address, so if a rider requests information, he may receive an answer or he may not, or he may receive it so late that it is no longer important.

Two associations that have permanent addresses are the NATRC at 1995 Day Road, Gilroy, California 95020; and the American Endurance Ride Conference, P.O. Box 1605, Auburn, California 95603. Also, information can be obtained from the Appaloosa Horse Club, P.O. Box 403, Moscow, Idaho 83843; and the International Arabian Horse Association, 224 East Olive, Burbank, California 91503.

Individual Rides such as the Vermont Ride, the Florida Ride, the Tevis, and the Bitterroot have permanent addresses which can be found, if it is difficult to get in touch with an Association, in the breed and horse magazines that can be purchased at any large book shop.   (There is one exception: *The Chronicle of the Horse,* which is sold by subscription only at Berryville, Virginia 22611.   *The Chronicle* runs short articles on Distance Rides and lists them in the Sporting Calendar.)   Other magazines are *Western Horseman* (Riding the Trails and Coming Events), *Horse and Horsemen, Appaloosa News, Arabian Horse News, The Morgan Horse.*   Nearly any equestrian magazine that is not devoted solely to one event, such as racing or horse shows, will contain information in columns, articles, or advertisements about Distance Rides.

The advantage of contacting a Conference or Association is that the contestant receives a list of sponsored Rides that will enable him to choose not one but any number of Rides in a location he desires, and to compete for a high-point trophy.   In addition, the contestant will be sure that the Ride will meet certain standards, or it would not have been accepted by the Conference to which it belongs.

But what if the contestant doesn't know which Ride to select?   To assist him in his choice, we will describe two of the better known Rides — the Virginia Competitive and the Tevis Endurance.

13. Virginia: The Gentleman's Ride

"THIS RIDE is planned for mid-April," the charming older woman explained, "at the end of the hunting season, when the horses are in condition. The distance is 40-40-20, the 100-mile total to be ridden in three days."

We were standing in front of The Homestead, the famous monument to southern hospitality, with its red brick and white-trimmed tower and semicircular wings on either side.

On the left, in a valley, we could see an immaculate golf course, tennis courts, and an enclosed swimming pool. A carriage, drawn by two horses, trotted past, but it was too cold for anyone but the trail riders to be out of doors. A bitter wind whipped the leafless trees. The judges huddled in their coats, while Tex, clutching her recording sheet, shivered as she watched the concrete road where the riders were due to appear.

The woman to whom I talked wore a coat and a felt hat that had grown comfortably shabby, as only good things can. She had, she said, been coming to The Homestead for years, and her grandfather had driven a coach and four from Richmond to the resort in the last century.

"I used to ride," she said, "but I'm too old now."

She didn't mention that she had won the 100-Mile Ride at one time on her hunter. At the Virginia Ride, people do not boast about their horses; most of the people know the horses and their performances.

"You can never tell what the weather will be like in April," the woman said. "Sometimes it is cold like this and sometimes it is quite warm. That is because it is in the mountains."

On the Virginia border, the mountains rise to ridges of 3400 to 4000 feet, thickly wooded with oak, elm, and pine.

The Ride started near the colonnaded entrance of the Homestead, and ended in the same place. The trails maintained by the Homestead and the

Forest Service, were wide and well-kept, and had gradual slopes, a few steep climbs, and miles of easy going in the valleys. Red, white, and blue arrows — one color for each day — marked the course.

Twenty-three riders were entered in the 100-Mile, and the same number in the 50-Mile; the latter, an easier event than the 100-Mile, is 20, 20, and 10. For the 50-Mile there were two expert lay judges, and for the 100-Mile, two veterinarians and one lay judge. Entries were open to stallions, mares, and geldings fourteen hands or over and four or more years old.

Awards were made on a basis of condition — 100 percent — with one-half penalty point per minute for being early or for-being late. A rider was eliminated if more than a half-hour late.

As in other Rides, drugs and stimulants were forbidden. The 50 Mile was scored 40 percent for manners; 35 percent for condition, and 25 percent for way of going. Many 50-milers graduated to the 100-Mile.

The Virginia Ride was started in 1958, which makes it the second oldest Ride in the east; Vermont is the oldest. It is governed by four officers and a board of stewards, and riders must be members of the Virginia Trail Riders Association. If sixty entries are not received, the members may nominate a rider over sixteen years of age who is acceptable to the Board of Stewards. That is to say, the Ride is by invitation only.

As I shivered at the finish line, watching the riders trot in one after another at the direction of the judges, I reflected that there were more than the average number of Thoroughbreds for an eastern Ride, certainly for a western event. With fingers numb with cold, I leafed through the program that listed the rider, owner, horse, sire, dam, and history of the horse. This is an amenity that many Rides might copy.

". . . thoroughbred bay gelding . . . 16.3 . . . raced. Hunted. 3 Virginia 50-Mile Rides."

". . . thoroughbred bay mare . . . 15.1 . . . hunter."

". . . bay mare . . . 15.3 hands . . . combined training. Preliminary division."

". . . hunter . . . raced. 3 wins."

". . . Maryland Horse of Year . . . stakes winner of $350,000 over jumps. Deep Pine Hunt."

There were also many Arabians. One mare, 15 hands, had been on ten

100-mile Rides in Florida, Virginia, Vermont, North Carolina, and Ohio. Her owner, a woman well-known on the eastern circuit, had ridden in more Rides than any competitor, and had placed well in all of them. She was one of the three in the Ride who had a western saddle.

Of added interest in the program was a list of previous winners, which included three Hungarians, a Moyle horse from Idaho, internationally known Thoroughbreds owned and ridden by Mr. Paul Mellon, and one horse whose breeding I did not know, but whose name was simply Idiot.

A number of Appaloosas were entered, half-breds and a Quarter Horse–Morgan gelding. One of the Appaloosas was described as a bay mare, 16.1 hands, a "novice at Competitive and Endurance trail rides." Her owner and rider was a Navy commander, and he also rode a western saddle, as did the young woman on a Quarter Horse–Morgan gelding.

From where we were standing, we could see some distance up the road, so that we could observe the horses the last half-mile before the finish. They walked as slowly as possible, and when the timer stopped them to prevent bunching up before the judges, many had to wait five or ten minutes. As a result, the horses came in in nearly the same shape they went out that morning. The judge's comments on the sheets were "bright," "damp," "brushing," "dehydrated," "slightly fatigued," "interfering," and so forth.

Few pulse and respiration readings were taken on the Ride. However, this did not prevent the judges from giving each horse a thorough examination at the check-in and during the hour checks each day after the finish. The judges knew the terrain and the types of horses. In addition, they had ridden the Virginia Ride, as well as numerous others. The same could be said about the two lay judges for the 50-Mile.

Pads were permitted, but leading was not. Starting time was 8:30.

According to the rules, time on the road was reckoned from "check out" at the start to "check in" at the finish. Horses could cross the finish line the first and second days of the Ride in not less than six hours thirty minutes, and not more than seven hours, without incurring penalty points. Horses taking more than seven hours thirty minutes were eliminated.

The lunch break was included in the riding time, which meant the riders grabbed a sandwich and went on.

"If you stop too long," one rider told me, "the horse loses his momentum."

This was a theory I had not heard before, but that I felt could bear investigation. The type of Ride would, of course, have some bearing on the matter.

A helper or groom was allowed to lead the horse around while the rider took the necessary break, but only the rider could loosen the cinch, bathe the horse's legs, or tend to the horse in any other way. Because it was cold, the horses were blanketed and no water was used.

The riders checked in on Monday and the examination held at the stables, which were located in the woods not far from The Homestead. The stables did not belong to the resort, and could have done with a little repair work, but they were large and bedding was provided, while there were plenty of water faucets and a parking area for trailers, campers, and trucks. Most of the contestants stayed at the Cascades Inn (American Plan), which is owned by The Homestead, and is six miles from the stables — a white, colonnaded building with a fireplace in the lobby and delightful, high-ceilinged rooms. Breakfast was served buffet — fresh strawberries, grapefruit, juice, cantaloupe, scrambled eggs in butter, toast and muffins, bacon, sausage, ham, and pots of excellent coffee. Cloths on the tables were white linen; during our stay at Hot Springs I never saw a paper napkin.

Monday night before the Ride a cocktail party and official dinner was held at the Homestead for "Members, Participants, and their guests by kind invitation of the President of The Homestead." The women wore long gowns. Indeed, every night the women dressed for dinner, although not as formally as for the banquet at the Homestead, which demanded special ceremony with its long, high-ceilinged dining room with arched windows along one side, immense chandeliers, and decor in pale green, gilt, and white. Fresh flowers on the tables and waiters in white coats, who placed before the guests shrimp cocktails, Niçoise salad, broccoli with hollandaise, beef done to the proper pinkness, peach melba, and petit fours from The Homestead's pastry chef.

The Homestead catered the noon stop, too, where a truck, overseen by a chef in a white cap and apron, offered hot soup, chicken and turkey sandwiches, fruit, coffee, and pastries.

If I dwell overlong on the amenities, it is because they are part of the Virginia Ride. The management emphasizes the atmosphere — not consciously so, but as a tradition — which might be one reason for the general attitude of sportsmanship. No one is determined to win at all costs, or is overly competitive. The sport itself is what matters, and the horse comes first. During hours of walking around the stables and watching the contestants at the various stops, I did not see a single rider mistreat his horse, and I saw one rider pull his mount when he thought it might be going lame. Indeed, I have seldom seen contestants take as good care of their animals. As soon as they returned to the stable after the finish of each day's ride, and before the hour check, they brushed, bathed, checked feet, and walked their horses. In the early morning, the rider or a friend who was helping, or a professional groom, was at the stable feeding and watering. Before that time, the horses were not allowed to be taken out of the stalls. From the last check to the start of the Ride on the following morning, the horses had to be left in their stalls and their riders could not go near them. A night watchman checked at intervals on each animal.

Only once did I hear riders complain, and that was the second day at noon lunch stop in a narrow valley, with timbered ridges rising on both sides and a deserted mansion in the center of the valley that looked like a relic of the Civil War. The riders had negotiated the stiffest climb of the day and come down a rocky decline.

A plump woman on a large chestnut, who surprised me by being such a capable horsewoman until I learned she was a joint master of one of the well-known hunts, snapped, "You'll have to change that trail. My horse had to cross his feet to get down. It's too steep and rocky."

The trail, compared to many in the west, was not steep or narrow, but the Virginia Ride is not a western Ride and it is a mistake to make comparisons. Indeed, it is a mistake to compare any Ride to another, for each is unique in terrain, climate, horses, riders, rules, and accommodations.

Awards are given on Thursday afternoon, following the finish of the third and last day of the Ride and lunch. Ribbons go to five places. The Champion and Reserve Champion are selected separately from those who place in the lightweight, middleweight, and heavyweight divisions. There is no junior division. A silver challenge bowl is presented by Mr. Paul Mellon and silver trophies go to the best hunter type, the best Arabian, and the best unregistered horse.

If I wanted to ride in a first Ride of the season, one that was not too tough and yet a fair test, I would select the Virginia Ride. Indeed, I might select it anyhow, for it has preserved what is vital to Competitive Rides — sportsmanship and the gentlemanly spirit of the amateur.

14. The Tevis: Test of Rider and Horse

IT WAS STILL dark and cold at a quarter to five in the morning when the riders gathered at the starting line in Squaw Valley. Tex (so she said later) could hardly believe that at last she was riding the famous Tevis. Shoulders hunched in her jacket, she shivered, partly from the chill in the mountain valley and partly because she was wondering if she could make the 100 miles across the Sierras to Auburn, California. Numbers of people failed, becoming so exhausted that they fell off their horses or, trying to continue, flopped in the saddle like scarecrows. Lacking the support of the rider, the horse became fatigued, too. The horse couldn't do it all, any more than the rider; the 100 miles had to be a cooperative effort between man and his mount.

Above all, Tex was afraid that the Flower Child would go lame on the rocks or would fall and be hurt. Horses had been injured on Endurance Rides; some had died, some had gone over the narrow trails and had to be hauled out of the canyons by helicopter. Pre-Ride nerves? The old, experienced riders confessed that even they suffered from the affliction. Tex wondered about the others in her party—Margit, who was riding Taszilo, a powerful bay; Lindy, who was on a dappled grey; and a trainer from California riding a grey gelding. Margit had ridden the Tevis once before, while the trainer had ridden it many times. According to pre-Ride plans, the trainer would assist Tex, Margit, and Lindy as much as possible.

Flower Child had been on several competitive Rides, but never an endurance ride. Tex had shown him as a hunter, and that was what he liked to do. Would he be uncooperative and ornery? Once or twice in training he had shown his dislike of trotting miles across country for no apparent purpose.

Tex looked around. How many entries were there? About 180? In the gloom, the dark shapes of horses and riders shifted like leaves in a current, bunching here, separating there. Hooves clattered on the pavement, horses snorted, riders called sharply as excited animals careened into them. The announcer shouted the time over a loudspeaker.

"Five minutes to go! Group One leaves in five minutes!"

The day before the riders had drawn for position in a group that included ten entries. Each group was to depart at two-minute intervals. Margit had drawn Group Five, the trainer Sixteen, and Tex had drawn Twenty, which meant she would be among the last to leave. If the Flower Child saw Taszilo depart, he would want to go too, so to quiet him, Tex drew away from the crowd and rode the Flower Child in a circle near the parked trucks, horse vans, and rows of shivering spectators. Flower Child's cream dun coat was clearly visible in the darkness; so, too, was an Albino horse, ridden by a girl in jeans and a visored cap, whom Tex recognized as a friend from home.

"I'm scared; are you?" the girl called.

"Sort of," Tex called back.

The girl and her mother had trucked the Albino 1200 miles. Tex's party had come as far, but they had a two-horse van, a camper, and a trailer loaded with hay, grain, and equipment. Among the crew was a professional truck driver and Bud, an experienced horseman and blacksmith. Success or failure depended to a large extent on the efficiency of the ground crew, although some of the riders who had done the Tevis many times, or who lived in the vicinity, scorned ground crews and took pride in making the 100 miles without help.

Tex's party had arrived at Auburn, where the stables were located, a week early in order to pre-ride part of the trail. The altitude was no problem; Tex and Margit had trained for months in the mountains, trotting for long distances at night and in the heat of the day. Also, warned of the rocks in the trail, they had shod their horses with pads. However, pads could wear out, and it was hotter in the Sierras than it was at home. Tex thrived in the heat, but what if, despite electrolytes, Flower Child became dehydrated? A 1000-pound horse has about 75 gallons of water in his body; Flower Child weighed 1100. Under severe stress (such as a 100-mile Ride over mountains in 24 hours), electrolyte imbalance could result in dehydration followed by exhaustion. This, in turn, could bring on thumps, tying-up, or colic that could, if not treated, promptly kill a horse.

Flower Child shook his head, pulling at the bit. He knew something was happening, and he didn't want to be left behind. If the other horses were going, he wanted to go, too.

"First Group! Go!"

In the growing light, Tex could see the riders trotting out and then, slowing to the climb up the steep slope that was a ski run in the winter, small, dark figures were strung out like beads against the immensity of the mountain.

"Group Five!"

Margit trotted out on Taszilo, and Flower Child, seeing his friend leaving, neighed loudly.

"Behave yourself, brat!" Tex admonished sternly, "or you'll wear yourself out before the start."

The horse, Tex thought, was in as good condition as he would ever be, well-muscled and with ribs just showing. Some of the mounts ridden by people who were going out to win looked like ganted-up race horses. There had been a good opportunity to see them the day before at the preliminary veterinary inspection at the Rodeo Arena in Squaw Valley. The sun had been hot, the arena had been dusty, as horses milled around — Arabians, Morgans, Mustangs, Appaloosas, Thoroughbreds, grade horses, Quarter Horses, a few Albinos, Moyles, Tennessee Walkers, Standardbreds, Hungarians, and one mule. Among the veterinarians were many whose names were well known in their profession, as well as veterinarians from other countries, who had come to the Tevis to see this test of horses under stress.

Also in the crowd were distance riders who had won the Tevis once or several times, or who had won the Haggin Cup for the best-conditioned horse among the first ten to arrive at the Auburn Fairgrounds. Donna and her husband, Pat Fitzgerald, were recognized by everyone as top contenders. Donna, an attractive blonde with tanned arms, was — so rumor went — going for another win on her gelding Witezarif, who had become a legend among Endurance horses.

The Flower Child had to see everything; his head was up, his amber-colored eyes rolling, his nostrils flaring. So excited was he that when his PR's were taken by one of the efficient PR teams, he had a pulse of 36 and respiration the same. Ordinarily his respiration was 14. Fortunately the vets were aware of how excitement heightens a horse's pulse and respiration, and when the Flower Child trotted a figure-eight perfectly, he was passed as fit. However, Tex had problems; she was too light, even with her 42-pound saddle. The minimum weight was 150 pounds, so she had to fill two canteens with water and tie a heavy jacket on the back of her saddle.

In the evening, after dinner, the pre-Ride briefing was held in Squaw Valley. The rules and the trail were reviewed. Tex liked the message from the Veterinary Examining Committee that read:

"We enjoy helping on the Ride because we like horses and endurance trail riding just like you. We hope that each of you is successful in obtaining a buckle [awarded to contestants who complete the 100 miles in the required time]. We will do all in our power to help obtain this goal. We believe, however, that you will agree that the horse's best interests come first."

Mr. Wendell Robie, president of the Western States Trail Ride (who had ridden the Tevis ten times), also told how the trail followed the route taken by miners and the Pony Express in the days of the gold rush, and how it has remained relatively unchanged. The grandson of Lloyd Tevis, president of Wells Fargo in the early days, awards the Tevis Cup, while the Haggin Cup, given for the best-conditioned horse, is awarded by the grandson of J. B. Haggin, early California mining magnate. The historical background of the Ride, the prominent people associated with it, and who have ridden it, give the Tevis a status that no other endurance Ride has in the country.

"The toughest test of horse and man in the world today!" declared one noted authority.

Who could resist such a challenge? To win the Tevis buckle is the supreme accomplishment.

The crowd at the starting line was thinning.

"Group Twenty! Go!"

The Flower Child started at a long, swinging trot. Instead of fighting him, Tex decided to let him take his own gait. Daylight was dispelling the shadows; Flower Child slowed, but continued to trot up the side of the mountain, passing several riders. Gradually the horse dropped to a walk, for the trail climbed 2700 feet from the valley to the summit of Emigrant Pass, which was above timberline. Here the trail led through barren rock and shale and snowbanks, with a view of distant peaks nine and ten thousand feet high, slashed by immense gorges. Tex could only glance at the spectacular panorama; that's all any rider on the Tevis could do, for the trail, timing, and horse demanded full attention. On the descent from the pass, Tex caught up with the trainer, who had left in Group Sixteen, and shortly afterward with Margit.

No conversation was possible; breath had to be saved for the trot, and occasionally for dismounting and running down the narrow trail, leading the horse. This eased concussion on the animal's legs, and also kept the rider limber, although only those in as good condition as their mounts could manage it. Down an open slope to Little American Valley, with white arrows painted on rocks to point the way. Red Star Ridge, and then the famous Cougar Rock, where the trail leads straight up the face of a cliff, with drops of hundreds of feet on both sides. The Flower Child looked at this obstacle, which seemed insurmountable; then, without pausing, he scrabbled up the cliff.

"That's a good boy!" Tex congratulated the gelding. He'd never refused a fence in a horse show, nor would he be intimidated by a cliff in the Sierras.

The trainer and a young man the trainer was helping to win his buckle were in the lead, then Lindy, Margit, and Tex. Tex felt that she and Margit might have trotted at a faster pace, but she said nothing, for the others were experienced and she was not. It was beginning to get warm, and the dust rose in clouds so that it was difficult to distinguish the rider ahead. Around the shoulder of a mountain and out on top of a ridge with mountain ranges as far as eye could see. More descents, and after that, comparatively level terrain where the trail was studded with rocks. The Flower Child crossed a huge slab of granite, slipped on the treacherous surface, and thudded onto his side. Sensing what was coming, Tex jerked her foot free of the stirrup, but she felt a stab of pain in her right knee. Immediately, the Flower Child struggled to his feet, snorting, but making no attempt to run away. Instead, he nuzzled Tex. He wasn't hurt. Tex breathed a sigh of relief, after she'd examined the horse's legs.

A contestant in jeans and a cowboy hat, trotting past, shouted, "Are you okay?"

"Fine!" Tex waved.

If Tex had needed help, she was sure the rider would have volunteered, although not everyone was willing to lose the chance for a buckle by assisting casualties. Contestants on Endurance Rides are supposed to look after themselves; not unreasonable, since months of training and considerable sums of money go into preparation for a Ride. The best Tex could have expected was for a rider to carry word ahead to the first checkpoint of an injury on the trail. But then she would be responsible for getting her horse to a place where he could be trailered to the stable. In other words, she was pretty much on her own.

Margit and the trainer were out of sight, riding at a trot in the haze of dust. Mounting, Tex turned the Flower Child into the trail and urged him to a trot. As she did so, she felt pain grab at her knee, and looking down, saw torn jeans and blood oozing from lacerated skin. It couldn't be helped; she'd have to wait until she got to Robinson Flat to attend to the injury.

All that mattered was that the Flower Child hadn't been hurt, and was eager to catch up to his friend, Taszilo. The trail was still rocky and the dust inches deep, but the open slopes of the mountains had become forests of ponderosa pine, whose shade was welcome after the glare of the sun. The first one-hour checkpoint, Tex knew, was Robinson Flat, which couldn't be far ahead. She passed two riders who were beginning to falter—a man and a woman—and then at a small stream, came up with Margit and the trainer, who were watering their horses and who went on, while Tex paused to give the Flower Child twelve swallows. The stream was only five or six miles from Robinson Flat. To make the 100-mile Ride in 24 hours, a contestant had to be at Robinson Flat Ranger Station no later than 2:30 P.M.; at Michigan Bluff, the next one-hour stop, by 7:45; and at Echo Hills, the third and last one-hour stop, by 1:00 A.M.

Robinson Flat, on the crest of a Sierra ridge, is an open meadow surrounded by pines. At the In gate, Tex was timed in and received a slip that told her which vet crew to report to. After the Flower Child had been checked, Tex led him to an area where the ground crew was waiting to sponge and feed the horses and let them rest apart from other horses, riders, timers, judges, PR teams, and helpers. The water used to sponge the horses was warm in the buckets; only the legs and faces were dampened, for the air was still chilly at the high altitude. A small amount of electrolytes was added to the grain and water to maintain the fluid balance. Flower Child's pulse was 74, respiration 36. Tex, knowing she had to remain in good shape to help the horse, tended to her knee, assisted by a member of the ground crew, who provided a first-aid kit. When the knee, which was beginning to swell, was bandaged, Tex had a sandwich and fruit.

"Well," Margit said, over a paper cup of coffee, "we only have about 65 miles to go."

Lindy smiled wanly; she had asthma, and the dust was bothering her, despite a nose mask.

The trainer said, "They're eliminating quite a few."

Horses were being rechecked by the veterinarians. If a horse's pulse did not fall below 70 and the respiration below 40, the horse was rechecked at the end of 45 minutes, again at 60, and after that, if he hadn't recovered, eliminated. At Robinson Flats a half-dozen riders withdrew voluntarily, and more were pulled by the veterinarians for lameness, poor recovery, fatigue, and dehydration. From now on the attrition rate would mount. Tex hoped that the Flower Child would not be among the unlucky ones, or any horses in her party.

Except for her knee, Tex felt fine. The heat did not bother her as it did some of the others, and she felt no need to take salt tablets. Margit, who could not take salt tablets, used Dolomite tablets. Margit was older than the other members in the group, but, with the exception of Tex, was in better shape than any of them, which proved that advance planning and training for rider, as well as horse, paid off. In addition, Margit had absorbed information for years on endurance riding, had read everything she could find on the subject, talked to veterinarians and riders, and watched endurance events, including the Tevis, before she had participated in her first event. An experienced horsewoman, she did not think she knew it all. This was an example that any rider might emulate, for riders or judges could testify that ignorance is the greatest cause of failure on the Tevis.

Both Tex and Margit wore jeans and broad-brimmed western hats, and beneath the jeans, light silk or cotton tights to prevent rubbing. Some of the riders, however, wore tank tops and no hats, which invited severe sunburn, if not heat stroke.

After the rest at Robinson Flat, the Flower Child trotted freely after Taszilo through a forest of ponderosa pines checkered by sunlight. At the Out check, the gelding's pulse had been 60 and respiration had been 12. Tex tried to estimate their riding speed; eight or nine miles at the trot? This was the best they had done, and they would be slowed down considerably by the canyons that lay ahead. All they could do was to make the fastest time possible on the good parts of the trail to compensate for the stretches where they had to walk or lead. The greatest difficulty was that they were unable to trot for long periods, but had to trot for a few hundred feet, then walk, then trot fifty feet, and walk again, which was not only physically wearing on the horse and rider but mentally exasperating.

From Robinson Flat the trail sloped gradually toward Last Chance, a cluster of weather-stained buildings that had been the site of a famous mine of the same name. At Last Chance, the handful of people who lived there served lemonade and held horses for those who needed a respite. To Tex, the lemonade was a welcome refreshment, and to Margit, too, who informed Tex that the Tevis was a big event to the inhabitants of Last Chance, and that every year they prepared lemonade for the riders.

Within a few minutes of leaving Last Chance, the oasis was only a memory, for the trail, narrow and eroded, switchbacked more than 2000 feet into the canyon of the North Fork of the Middle Fork of the American River. To glance over the side of the trail, barely wide enough for a horse, was to court giddiness. The sun glared; the temperature hovered toward ninety. Puffs of dust against the barren flank of the mountain showed where riders were walking or leading their horses. Margit and Tex dismounted, and Tex, setting her teeth against the ache in her knee, led the Flower Child at a half-run down the switchbacks, slowing on the sharp turns so that the gelding could see where he was going; a misstep and he could crash over the cliffs into the canyon.

When they reached the river, they watered the horses and Tex sponged Flower Child hastily, while the others did the same for their mounts. Then they were off again, across a suspension bridge and up 2000 feet from the Middle Fork. Ahead, a rider was tailing his horse, but neither Tex nor Margit emulated his example. They were not heavyweights, and Tex had to care for her knee if she hoped to complete the Ride. At the rim of the canyon, they came out to the Devil's Thumb, where the veterinarians were waiting for a thirty-minute check. The Flower Child's pulse was 68 and his respiration 68, which was not good. A number of other horses ridden by other contestants showed signs of extreme fatigue, and were eliminated, while some riders withdrew on their own, preferring to trailer out, rather than continue into the canyons that lay ahead. Bud Dardi, ex-winner of the Tevis, was pulled for fatigue. One man collapsed on heat-withered grass, his face grey from exhaustion. A girl sobbed against her horse's flank, "I can't go on! I can't go on!"

Another man, bending over his horse's front foot, complained unhappily that he had lost a shoe.

"You can borrow one of our boots," Margit told him, and gave the man a plastic boot that fit over the horse's foot and tied above the pastern — an equestrian spare tire with which Tex and Margit were provided in case of emergency.

How many horses had been eliminated so far? There was no way to tell, but Tex felt better when the Flower Child's pulse fell to 48 and his respiration to 25 on the Out check. Leaving the Devil's Thumb, Tex and her companions began another long descent by switchback, 3000 feet into El Dorado Canyon. Horses and riders were filmed with dust, faces caked with it. Tex could feel the grit in her teeth. The heat enveloped, smoth-

ered. Tex and Margit jogged halfway down, leading their horses, knowing, as did all experienced Endurance riders, that it is more difficult for a
tired horse to go downhill than up. Tex, wondering about riding speed,
looked at her watch from dust-rimmed eyes, but the heat, the pain in her
knee, and a growing tiredness fogged her mind so that she gave up trying
to figure how many miles they had come in how many hours, and how
many miles remained to be ridden.

The river again, and a drink for the horse and another quick sponging.
Tex would have liked to dive into the water, but there was no time. Up
again, 2000 feet through scrub oak and brush to — Thank God, at
last! — Michigan Bluff. Lindy's horse lagged, and Lindy, too, was suffering. Tex hoped she could go on, for the girl had courage.

At Michigan Bluff, PR teams, veterinarians, and spectators lined the
one street of the old mining town that had been built atop the ridge
among oaks and manzanita. Many riders were already in. Those going
for the Top Ten had left. Who were they? Their names were on everyone's lips — Donna Fitzgerald. Nick Mansfield. Hal Hall.

Flower Child's pulse in was 68; respiration 32, which was good, considering the steep climbs. Lindy's horse had an In pulse of 80 and respiration of 72, which was not encouraging. Numbers of other horses were
eliminated for lameness, thumps, and exhaustion.

The trainer, a talented horsewoman, did not want to lose a horse. At
her direction, the neck and croup of Lindy's grey and the horse ridden by
the lanky young man were draped with wet gunny sacks, and the horses
led around slowly. Every five minutes they were allowed three sips of
water. After twenty minutes the trainer took the PR's and declared they
were down — not as much as could be wished, but down enough so that
the veterinarians would not hold or eliminate the horses.

While the horses were being attended to by the ground crew, the riders
stretched gratefully on blankets to sip juice and eat fruit and cold chicken.
Everywhere among the decaying wooden buildings and oak trees, horses
were munching hay or being sponged off. Riders lay flat on their backs
while others ate or led their horses about, or stood waiting to be called for
the second vet check. The sun was slanting low in the west, and the
shadows were beginning to lengthen. An hour is not very long, and Bud
had to work fast to replace the plastic pads, which had been splintered by
the rocks, on the Flower Child's front feet.

Food, a face wash and a clean shirt did much to revive Tex. A
member of the ground crew renewed the bandage on her knee and handed

her a flashlight, as she took Flower Child's reins to lead him to the Out check. Pulse 60; respiration 16. From Michigan Bluff, the trail descended a thousand feet into Volcano Canyon, and then up toward Forest Hills, a small town on a timbered plateau. By this time it was dark, and the lights were on in the gas stations and small shops that bordered the highway. For several miles the riders trotted on the pavement, pausing to let their horses drink water provided for them in containers in the center of town. Here Tex's friend on the Albino caught up with them, and joined the party, explaining that her previous companion had decided on a faster pace than she could maintain.

After leaving Forest Hills, still trotting in the dark, the riders turned off the highway by a ranger station and followed a trail black-shadowed by pines, downhill to an abandoned road where heaps of gravel were all that remained of early-day hydraulic diggings. The Flower Child trotted when Tex asked him to, but he was not the eager charger he had been, nearly seventeen hours before. Nor was Tex as fresh as she had been. Down once more to the river and up toward the last one-hour vet check at Echo Hills. Within a mile or so of Echo Hills, Taszilo stumbled and fell to his knees. Pulling him up, Margit dismounted, and while Tex held the flashlight, she examined the bay's leg, which was badly cut. However, the bone was not damaged.

Fearful of losing riding time, Tex's friend went on with a group of riders whose identity was lost in the darkness, while Tex's party rode in at a walk. At Echo Hills Ranch, where lights blazed on the veterinary checkpoint, Margit declared that she was pulling Taszilo, although the vets said the gelding could continue.

"My horse is too important to risk bringing him in lame," Margit declared.

Her voice reflected her disappointment. To have come more than seventy miles and then be unable to go on was a blow, but that was a risk every rider took when he entered the Tevis.

At Echo Hills, the Flower Child's pulse was 44 In; respiration 16; Out, pulse 40; respiration 12. But Lindy's horse was eliminated for thumps.

So Tex, the trainer, and the young man were the three remaining of the party. Leaving the lights of the vet check, they rode into the darkness on a continuing downhill grade to the river, where the horses drank, and then a climb up the opposite ridge. Once again the river was crossed, this time on a bridge sixty feet above the water that had no guard rail. In daylight, the bridge would have been difficult to negotiate; in the blackness of a clouded night, when a horse could shy and go over the side, it was frightening. The Flower Child snorted, but he did not object to crossing. On the opposite bank, the trail followed an old railroad grade, and here Tex left the trainer and the young man, whose horses were beginning to lag, and rode alone. Ordinarily, the Tevis is held during the full moon, so that the riders can see the trail better at night, but this year the sky was overcast; not even a star glimmered through the clouds. Abruptly, the Flower Child stopped. Tex tried to knee him forward, but he would not move. Switching on the flash, Tex saw a washout which, if the Flower Child had not sensed it, they would have crashed into head over heels.

At the bottom of the canyon, lights signaled a fifteen-minute vet check, which the Flower Child passed satisfactorily. As Tex came into the check, she saw her friend with the Albino just leaving.

"Do you think we'll make it in time?" the girl asked.

"If we hurry," Tex replied. "We don't have far to go now."

From the canyon the trail climbed to Robie Point and a final veterinary inspection. At this stop, the trainer was held over for fifteen minutes, while Tex, still riding alone, continued the last few miles in what had now become early morning darkness. Somehow the Flower Child sensed he was nearly home, for he strode out at a fast walk, passing numerous riders urging tired horses down the streets of Auburn and across the railroad tracks. Beneath the underpass, and then into the Fairgrounds and around the track to the finish line in front of the floodlit grandstand.

They'd made it!

Tex didn't know whether to laugh or cry. She wasn't aware of her exhaustion; her thought was for the Flower Child, whose willingness and sagacity had brought them through. Only a horseman can understand the ecstasy of such a moment.

Refusing to let anyone else attend to her mount, Tex led the Flower Child to his stall, sponged, watered, and fed him, and then left him to lie down, with a sigh, on the pile of fresh straw. After a hundred miles across the Sierras, a horse needs rest.

The next day the Flower Child was fit to ride again. Tex had done the Ride in 19 hours 45 minutes. Donna Fitzgerald, who won the Tevis Cup, made the 100 miles on her eight-year-old Arabian gelding in a total riding time of twelve hours and 52 minutes, but she did not wear her buckle with more pride than Tex. This buckle cannot be bought for any price; to wear it, a person has to earn it the hard way.

15. After the Ride: Period of Adjustment

IF A PERSON wants to continue riding a distance horse, he must take as good care of him after the Ride as before, and the time to start is at the finish line.

The rider is tired; he would like to shove the horse into a stall and go off somewhere to lie down, preferably with a cold beer and a comrade to rub his aching muscles with Absorbine.

A contestant in a 1922 Endurance Ride, a cowboy, groaned, ''I have ridden sixty miles a day lots of times, but this is the first time I ever rode sixty *measured* miles.''

In the days of the Cavalry, the Infantry taunted that elite branch by reminding them that the foot soldier only had to look after himself, but that the cavalryman had to care for his horse and then for himself. The same rule holds true for the distance rider. The horse comes first.

It might be helpful for the novice to know, in detail, how Tex cared for Voodoo after the Bitterroot Ride, which is a Competitive event and one that a novice would be more apt to enter than a 100-mile Endurance Ride such as the Tevis. Actually, the care is much the same for Competitive and Endurance Rides.

When Tex rode through the in gate at noon, she dismounted, and loosening the cinch, led Voodoo to the PR team and the veterinarian for the required check. As soon as the examination was finished, Tex exchanged Voodoo's bridle for a halter, and with the mare still saddled to keep pressure on her back and prevent heat bumps, led Voodoo around for fifteen minutes. By that time, Voodoo was beginning to cool down, so Tex unsaddled her, covered her with a light blanket, and, since it was a warm day, bathed the mare's legs with tepid water and sponged her head, nostrils, and lips. Taking off the blanket, she then sponged Voodoo's body, ministrations that the mare acknowledged by putting her head down to nuzzle Tex. Voodoo is not an affectionate animal, but even she wanted to show that horses appreciate attention following a hard workout.

After this, Tex walked the mare until she was dry and completely cool, pausing at intervals to allow her to graze or take a few sips of water. Most Rides require an hour check by veterinarians after completion of the event, so, with this in mind, Tex massaged the mare's legs and body as she had the previous day, although Voodoo did not appear to be stiff and only normally tired. The currycomb, brush, and cactus cloth completed the grooming, which must have been efficient, for Voodoo passed the check with good marks, or, at least, better than she would have if she had not been groomed, massaged, grazed, and watered.

The check over, Voodoo was put in a box stall with fresh bedding, given a little hay and a bucket of water, and left to rest. At 2:30 and again at five o'clock, Tex led her around for fifteen minutes, allowing her to graze and move at will. At 5:30 Tex fed her more hay and two pounds of grain, which the mare consumed with gusto, an encouraging sign, for exhausted or sick horses go off their feed.

On this Ride, the horses were allowed to be cared for at night, since high altitude caused sharp fluctuations in the temperature. By ten o'clock, it was cold and Tex blanketed Voodoo.

On Rides where we had competed that did not allow care at night, we had to rely on the night watchman if a horse got colicky or in some other trouble that demanded the owner's presence or that of a veterinarian. When medication is administered, the horse is eliminated from competition, no matter how well he might have done on the trail.

Early the following morning, Tex cleaned the stall and fed Voodoo a small amount of hay and half the grain ration. Rules prohibited taking the horse out of the stall two hours before the final check, which is required by the majority of Rides whether they are one-day, thirty-mile events or three-day events of a longer distance. The purpose of this check is to see if the horse is fit to continue on the trail. As a sponsor of the military Endurance Rides explained, the selection is based on the condition of the horse, judged by his suitability at the finish of the test, to proceed on another such test.

The examination was thorough, the veterinarians inspecting to see if the mare had cleaned up her feed and how she moved when she was led outside, where she was given a complete going over and then made to trot in a straight line, and after that, a figure eight, with Tex leading at the halter. The mare was a little stiff coming out of the stall, but moved, so Tex was glad to see, freely at the trot.

When the judges went on to the next horse, Tex took Voodoo a short distance from the stable where she allowed her to graze. Then she mucked out the stall so that the management would not be left with complaints from the fair board or have to pay to clean a dirty stable. This, again, is something that is frequently neglected by contestants.

At the awards ceremony that followed the final check and the judging, Voodoo placed fourth in the Lightweight Division, which pleased Tex, for the competition had been tough, although Voodoo only cast a bad-tempered eye at the ribbon when Tex showed it to her. She'd had enough of the Ride and wanted to go home, so Tex, knowing that the mare was well rested, wrapped Voodoo's legs, blanketed her, and loaded her into the trailer, where a little hay waited in the feed bunk, but no oats, since Voodoo developed nerves in a trailer and might colic if she had grain.

For once Voodoo rode quietly. At home, the blanket and leggings were taken off and the mare walked a short distance and then turned into the paddock. The following day, Voodoo was allowed to rest. She was not going to compete the remainder of the summer, so she had to be de-conditioned, which was done by reducing the grain and exercising the mare a half hour or so every day, gradually cutting the rides to once or twice a week and grain to a pound a day. As long as the weather remained pleasant, the mare was ridden as a pleasure horse; when it snowed, we pulled Voodoo's shoes, a routine practice on western ranches, and one that is recommended for hunters, for horses who are stabled all the time, and for animals in paddocks or pastures. Pulling the shoe is similar to taking the shoes off of a human and walking around in bare feet; circulation is improved and the removal of restrictions allows the foot to grow and function normally.

The remainder of the winter Voodoo spent in a pasture with other horses, where she could exercise and eat the hay which we pitched out twice a day.

The next season, Voodoo, as well as the other horses, would be experienced campaigners, while we had learned a great deal.

No real horseman stops learning; indeed, the way to tell the "true article" from the "fake" is that the former listens and says little, while the latter talks loudly and refuses to acknowledge that any way but his is the best. To the "fake," the trophy is all that counts. He is apt to load his horse immediately after the finish of the Ride and start for home. If he is eliminated or pulled, he will do the same. He can't win, so why hang around? This attitude reflects poor sportsmanship; in the end, the horse will pay for it.

The "fake" is too callous to realize that experience is more valuable than a plated silver tray. Not only has his horse been tested on the Ride, but horses in general.

The conclusions reached after some of the military Endurance trials might prove enlightening in this respect, and are as sound today as they were when written.

"Depending upon the weather and the heat of the horse, it is best to wait five or ten minutes before blanketing, for if the blanket is put on too soon, the horse can cool out too slowly and might break into a secondary sweating, while if the blanket is put on too late, the horse can become chilled and stiffen."

"The horses that placed the best at the finish had received approximately one year of conditioning, but the conditioning had not been carried to the point where the horse became stale. During this training period, it was important that the rider understood the accumulation of fatigue in horses; in other words, when the horse was tired and on the verge of being over-trained."

In *Elements of Hippology,* prepared for the Department of Tactics, United States Military Academy, Maj. F. C. Marshall wrote, "The horse should never be pushed to the limit of his endurance."

These findings, it should be remembered, were for 300- and 150-mile Endurance tests.

"A little fat over the hard muscles serves as a nerve feeder and adds to the recuperative power of the horse."

"The rider who was able to get off and lead finished much less tired than if he'd had to remain in the saddle during the contest." Again, this was for an Endurance trial.

The present-day distance rider, like the cavalryman, knows that a horse might finish with little sign of fatigue and no sweating. The rider, thinking the horse does not need cooling out, will put him in the stall and feed and water him, not realizing that the animal is still hot internally. Within a few hours the horse develops colic.

Stocking is another problem that affects horses after training or hard riding, who are put in a stable, overfed, and not exercised. The legs swell, in most cases below the knee, and while the condition is not as serious as colic or azoturia, it can cause temporary lameness. Massage, light exercise, and bandages can relieve stocking. Also, the feed should be cut down.

Injuries such as cuts, abrasions, muscle soreness, and some lamenesses will show up immediately after a Ride; splints, wind puffs, and spavins may not appear for some time, so it is advisable to check the horse's legs at intervals. As an aid to soreness and lameness, a number of riders advocate "boots" that come to the horse's knees and can be filled with water that is circulated with a small pump. If desired, Epsom salts can be added to the bubbling liquid.

But attention should not be directed entirely to the physical letdown of the horse. There is also the psychological aspect, and this, I am afraid, is sadly neglected by contestants through ignorance or carelessness.

All of our horses went through a period of readjustment; however, Flower Child showed his problems more plainly than the others. We saw him after the Tevis standing in the paddock, slack-hipped, his head down, suffering from the affliction common to retired athletes and business and professional men—boredom. The medical profession recognizes the depression that retirement brings to humans, but not many people realize that it can affect horses.

No longer was the Flower Child groomed twice a day, ridden twenty miles, and fed special supplements. While conditioning for the Tevis was hard, the Flower Child thrived on it and his physical well-being was reflected by his alertness. A healthy animal, like a healthy human, is mentally more responsive than a sluggish one.

Boredom leads to bad habits, such as chewing on the fence rails, laying back the ears when someone comes in the paddock, and jealousy. One day when it threatened rain and I was going to ride, Tex blanketed Mazda so that his back would not be wet when I saddled him. The Flower Child, whom Tex had had little time to ride since the Tevis, watched the operation, and then, walking straight to the tack room, clumped inside (which he had never done before), and, grabbing a blanket with his teeth from the rack, threw it on the floor. If Mazda was going to be blanketed, he should be, too.

When Tex left for school, Flower Child was not ridden at all, and I turned him out to pasture, for an idle horse is happier if he can move around and graze than he is if he is shut in a stable or paddock. If a horse must be kept in a small area, he should be able to see other horses, dogs or chickens, or even people. No human likes to be shut in a small room without windows, or confined in a fenced enclosure; why should a free-roaming animal like a horse?

To many people, it might seem foolish to cater to a horse's mental problems. If a horse remains sound after the Ride, he will be a good and obedient mount; what more is necessary? The answer to this is: what do you want? A horse that will give a mediocre performance, or one that will win? For the horse that is treated as a machine will remain a machine, while the horse who is not only groomed and ridden, but is also talked to and treated as an individual, will respond to his rider with all of his heart.

16. Dedicated Men:
The Veterinary Judges

IN THE FINAL analysis, the well-being of the horses on a Ride depends on the veterinarian judges assisted by lay judges, PR teams, recorders, and timers. The veterinarians determine if the horses are sufficiently sound to compete, if they are fit to continue the Ride, and where they place after the finish.

This is not an easy task. Indeed, most riders do not realize the concentration and physical effort involved. Whatever a veterinarian receives as a fee is a poor reward for his services, but most veterinarians do not judge for the money; they do it because they are interested in seeing what horses do under stress. Some judges, like Drs. Richard Barsaleau and B. C. Throgmorton of California, and Mathew Mackay-Smith and Clarence Parks of Pennsylvania (to name a few), not only judge, but they compete in Rides themselves, so that they have a first-hand understanding of conditioning and riding.

However, a veterinary degree does not necessarily qualify a person to judge distance rides. The *Guideline Manual of the Eastern Competitive Trail Ride Association* states the matter succinctly:

"Small animal veterinarians (regardless of willingness) rarely have the background to be competent for this specialized judging, and "Horse Show" judges are completely inadequate in this field."

A veterinarian might have other handicaps as well. Some years ago in a part of the country where distance riding was new, the local veterinarian was asked to judge. Not only was the good doctor elderly, but his face was red and his gait uncertain from alcoholic intake. His idea of a Competitive Ride was as vague as the management's, who left it to him to make the rules.

"We'll weigh the horses," the doctor declared, "and the horse that loses the least, wins. We got one a' them squeeze cattle pens around here for weighing, don't we?''

When the handful of terrified horses had been forced into the small, metal-barred pen, one of them injuring himself when he tried to rear, the doctor announced that that was enough for the preliminary check.

''Aren't you going to take my horse's pulse and respiration?'' one of the riders inquired.

''Ah, to be sure, to be sure,'' the doctor said; and placing his stethoscope against the horse's flank, leaned down to get the heart beat. Unfortunately, once in this position he was unable to rise, until, after some minutes, a rider assisted him to stand upright.

With the growing popularity of distance riding, the American Association of Equine Practitioners nominated a committee to publish *A Guide for Veterinary Judges of Competitive Trail and Endurance Rides.* In addition, the North American Trail Ride Conference prints a *Judge's Manual;* the Rocky Mountain Competitive Trail Ride Association includes *Veterinary Judging Criteria* in a booklet; the ECTRA issues information for judges while individual Rides, such as the Florida Ride and the Old Dominion 100-Mile Endurance Ride in Virginia, do the same.

This is a great help to judges who are not familiar with the rules, as well as to riders who like to know how their horses will be evaluated.

According to the *Guide for Veterinary Judges,* the veterinarian's first responsibility is to safeguard the horses; secondly, to estimate and score the horses on the Ride; and thirdly, to answer questions or proffer advice to interested individuals.

At all times the veterinarian is to remain impartial; keep his temper; and compromise with other judges, with whom he may not agree. He should be considerate of his recorder and PR team, which several well-known judges fail to do, earning themselves a reputation that makes volunteers reluctant to work with them.

Also, it is not the veterinarian's responsibility to make up rules during the Ride, but to abide by those established by the management.

Of equal importance is the veterinarian's relations with the competitors, which depends on his being a friendly authority. Some veterinarians fit the role easily, because they are naturally outgoing and have a sense of humor. Others are shy, or overcome by their importance, or impatient by nature, or annoyed at the management. These personal feelings are best forgotten while the veterinarian attends to his job, which is to evaluate the horses, and, to a degree, the riders, for frequently a judge's decision to pull a horse or let him continue depends upon the rider's skill or lack of it.

For whatever reasons people ride, they cannot help learning about horses, and, to a large extent, how much they learn is due to the veterinarian who takes time to answer questions: Why was my horse marked down for way of going at the check-in? Why was he held over at the lunch stop? Why do you have a fifteen-minute recovery period?

The veterinarian should not be expected to give a complete, clinical examination of a horse. If there are serious problems, he can sketch them to the rider and suggest he see his vet at home. Nor should the veterinarian keep other competitors standing around at the check-in while he discusses one individual's horse; it is more tactful to tell that person to see him at some other time.

Experienced veterinarians know what to look for at the preliminary check. After the horse has had his PR's taken, he is led out at halter. The NATRC Rides count horsemanship points in how the horse is presented; other Rides do not. The judge is not looking for a certain breed or conformation, except as it affects way of going. I have seen Endurance horses with their ribs showing and tincture of violet smeared over skinned places on legs and rumps; horses that would have placed highly in shows, but that were too wide behind or whose feet were too small for hard work on the trail. And I have seen narrow-chested, small-boned runts that I would not want to own, but that still placed first.

Horses, like people, react differently in crowds. Some will become excited; some, who are herd-bound, will neigh loudly. In these cases, the veterinary judge knows the pulse and respiration will be above normal rest.

In a Ride that judges 40 percent on soundness, 50 percent on condition and 10 percent on manners, the breakdown is as follows:

On soundness, cinch and saddle sores are scored according to severity. The horse that is "off" or stiff, or has some peculiarity of gait should be noted. If the horse is definitely lame, of course, he should not be allowed to compete.

On condition, half of the 50 percent is for PR's, while the remaining half is for an objective view of the horse.

Dr. D. P. Hatfield, Rocky Mountain and Canadian judge, and also a visiting judge at the Tevis, described the judge's evaluation as follows: (Dr. Hatfield is a tall, dark-haired young man with a flashing smile and tactful manner, which makes him popular with competitors.)

"The objective view of the horse (visual condition) is very important, and requires a lot of concentration and observation to assess accurately. No one sign can be used alone to evaluate a horse, but the combination of the following should accurately measure fatigue:

Scleral injection	Expression of eye
Relaxation of the anus	Dehydration
Capillary filling time	Presence of muscle tremors
Alteration in muscle flexion	Willingness to eat
Willingness to trot	Movement at the walk

"At the preliminary examination, the following signs referring to condition are noted:

"Scleral injection for each animal. Some horses may have injection from eye irritation, but this should not be confused later in the Ride as fatigue injection.

"Capillary filling time is indicated by pressing on the gum and watching the blood rush back. Some horses will have slowed capillary filling time at the start of the Ride, which should be marked down for further reference.

"Dehydration is evaluated by lifting a pinch of skin at the side of the neck and watching how quickly it springs back.

"A comment should be made on the judge's sheet as to how well the horse leads at the trot. A horse that leads poorly may be inaccurately judged as reluctant to trot out at the final check.

"Some system of classifying each horse as to movement and attitude should be made at this point, so the judge can refer to it later for any change caused by the stress of the Ride. For example, a hot-blooded horse may have a long, swinging trot at the preliminary examination, but when he becomes fatigued on the Ride, he may drag. On the other hand, a short, choppy-gaited horse may maintain the same way of going at the finish of the Ride as he did at the start. Thus, the gait will tell the judge a great deal about the effects of stress."

As a final word, Dr. Hatfield said, ". . . at this initial check, be sure to identify any horse you think will have difficulty in maintaining the pace of the Ride. Then be sure to look at these horses closely at the first stop, as there is rarely time to thoroughly evaluate every horse at this check."

Veterinarians pay particular attention to the legs and feet, which take much of the stress on Rides. The tendons should be firm, the fetlocks and pasterns free of scabs caused by interfering. When the hoof is pinched with the hoof testers, the animal should not flinch. Naturally, not all horses will be physically perfect. Some will have wind galls (swelling just behind and above the fetlock joint) that can mean hard usage; or a bowed tendon that might not make the horse lame; or he might show slight signs of brushing. These horses should be watched, but not disqualified at the preliminary check. Also, a veterinarian will often hear a heart murmur or third heartbeat through his stethoscope, which might confuse the PR team, but which is normal for that horse.

If a horse is to be eliminated at the preliminary check, it is advisable for two or more judges to discuss the matter before rendering a decision. Reasons for elimination, listed by *A Guide for Veterinary Judges,* are genuine lameness, sickness, respiratory trouble such as emphysema, evidences of hard usage (stiffness or inflammatory edema), severe cinch sores, badly cracked hooves, and loose shoes. In this latter case, a horse can be re-shod and brought back for approval.

While the judge is making his examination, he is telling his recorder (or secretary) what to write down, and from time to time on the Ride, he will ask the recorder what his observations were on a certain horse. He can't remember the details of every animal on the Ride, so it is important that the recorder list the judge's remarks concisely. During the final evaluation, the horses will be placed according to the information on these sheets.

At the briefing the night before the Ride, the veterinarian usually gives a short talk on the reasons the horses will be eliminated; how long the horses must remain in their stalls or tied up in the camping area at night; and how the weather will affect the riding time. The terrain and the type of Ride—Endurance or Competitive—will influence the judge's decisions in many respects.

"The judge's schedule," Dr. Hatfield wrote, "should be arranged so that at least one veterinarian or experienced non-vet judge sees every animal at every check point. It is usually impossible for a judge to see all the horses at all the points, due to distance and time involved in getting there."

Some veterinarians are not enthusiastic about lay judges, particularly if they are female.

"Let's face it," a well-known member of the profession told me, "veterinarians are misogynists."

Veterinarians feel that women lack the strength to handle large animals, and that, male or female, a lay judge is not qualified to give a clinical examination, which is true, but a knowledgeable horseman can tell a great deal about an animal. In fact, a person who has spent his life around horses might spot things that a veterinarian would not. Happily, in the majority of cases, the veterinarians are glad to serve with experienced laymen, and when those laymen are among the best known in the field, such as Alexander Mackay-Smith of Middleburg, Virginia, and Sharon Saare of the Appaloosa Horse Club, they defer to them on many matters.

When I serve as a lay judge, I keep in mind (being a female) that I must never tell the veterinarian his business, which would be very tactless indeed. I consider the veterinarian the senior judge and accept his decisions on soundness. With few exceptions, my evaluations differ little from the veterinarians', and I believe this is true in the cases of other lay judges.

One significant advantage of most lay judges is that they are volunteers, or are paid a minimal amount. The Ride might need two judges, but cannot afford to pay more than one veterinarian.

Whatever the case, I never cease to be impressed by the thorough examination that the veterinarians give the horses at the preliminary check. The vets might learn a great deal about stress on Rides, but the riders receive a "physical" for their horse that is worth many times more than the entry fee. In addition, the riders are given an abbreviated course in horse care.

Before the start of the Ride, the veterinarian has been told by the management how many checkpoints there are on the trail, and where they are located. A checkpoint at the top of a steep climb is a favorite, since it demands more effort than trotting on the level. On Endurance Rides and many Competitive Rides, PR's are taken at the noon lunch stop at the beginning and end of an hour, but on many Competitive Rides, this has been changed to a fifteen-minute check after arrival, since a horse's pulse and respiration will drop to normal within sixty minutes, unless the stress has been great and the horse has real problems. On an Endurance Ride, the horse has many miles to go over rough terrain; he needs the longer rest period. But on a Competitive Ride, the stress is not extreme, and if PR's are taken at hourly intervals, they are of little use for evaluation.

During the Ride, the veterinarian is watching for symptoms of fatigue which are manifested by visual signs as well as PR's. In the informative booklet issued by the Florida Horsemen's Association for the Florida

Ride, there is this quotation: "The cardinal sign heralding the onset of fatigue and eventual exhaustion is the PR ratio 1:1."

Also symptomatic is the case where the at-rest pulse and respiration on the third morning of a three-day 100-mile Ride (such as the Florida Ride) are higher than they were the first and second mornings.

The veterinarian keeps this in mind, as well as other signs of fatigue. Dr. S. J. Roberts of the Cornell Veterinary College, Ithaca, New York, lists some as follows:

- Distressed facial expression
- Posturing to urinate without producing urine
- Colicky signs
- Extreme stiffness of loins and croup muscles
- Excessive sweat, which may signify "tying up"
- Lack of sweat combined with high temperature

The veterinarian's responsibilities increase with the difficulty of the Ride. He might be alone at a checkpoint with his PR team and recorder and forty horses. Some of the horses are borderline cases. Should he allow them to continue or eliminate them? He can hold the doubtful ones over for a fifteen-minute recheck, but this does not always solve the problem. The veterinarian has to consider the trail that lies ahead. Are there steep climbs, long distances before the next checkpoint? If he cautions the rider to take it easy, will the rider heed the warning or ignore it? The decisions must be made quickly, and they are up to the veterinarian alone.

Nor does the veterinarian's responsibility end there. After the Ride he must be on the lookout for colic, lameness, and the various illnesses that affect animals after a period of stress. Also, he must conduct a one-hour check after the finish, and another the following morning. When this is done, he must place the horses. Various Rides that belong to various organizations have their rules for judging. They are all fair; politics and personal preference play no part in the decisions. Many times I have sat in at a judging where the veterinarians and lay judges have given the championship to a horse they definitely did not like, but which proved to be the soundest animal on the Ride and the best able to continue the following morning. Sometimes hours are devoted to comparing horses and PR's. The results at every checkpoint must be studied; the opinion of each judge must be considered and a compromise reached; and all this after hours of bouncing around the country in a four-wheel-drive vehicle, standing for lengthy periods while checking horses, and many times shivering in the cold or sweating in the heat.

To all intents and purposes, the veterinarian should be able to relax when the final trophy has been decided, but this is not the case. No sooner are the awards made by the management than the riders descend on the judge. Why didn't my horse place? Why did you mark my mare down at the second check? Do you think I should change my horse's feed? Would he do better if I gave him electrolytes?

This is the reason that distance ride judges are known as dedicated men; they have to be.

17. What We Are Looking For: The Lay Judges

Too OFTEN competitors are evaluated only by local judges whose equestrian experience is limited. This does not mean the judges do not know their business, but that they and the riders can benefit from a guest judge from another part of the country. The locals might not agree with the guest judge in every respect; this is not necessary. What is important is that they cannot help learning something, even if it is only that things are done differently elsewhere.

The more varied a judge's background, the more he has to offer, and this applies to lay judges as well as veterinarians.

Perhaps the top lay judge in the country is Alexander Mackay-Smith of Virginia. Not only is Mr. Mackay-Smith familiar with Olympic competition, he is a scholar as well, an authority on the Cleveland Bay and the Colonial Quarter Horse, and editor of *The Chronicle of the Horse*. His co-judge is frequently his attractive wife, Marilyn, who hunts and competes in Distance Rides. They do not always agree, which is as it should be, for decision is reached by compromise.

The several times I watched the Mackay-Smiths judge, the veterinarians who were working with them felt they put too much emphasis on breed and conformation, but when the Ride was finished, they admitted to an enlightening experience.

When I asked the Mackay-Smiths what they looked for at the preliminary examination, this is the answer I received:

"Instead of putting the emphasis on faults, we look first for the horses which seem to us the most capable of accomplishing the ride ahead. First we look at the way the horse moves, both from the side and from the front and rear, and at both walk and trot. Viewing from the side, we want a horse that moves freely from his shoulders and stifles, active at both gaits, one whose hind feet at the walk overstep the prints of the front feet by several inches. At the trot we like a horse who points his front feet well forward, and who also has good use of his hocks, lifting them up and forward. When viewed from the front and back, the horse should travel straight, the prints of the hind legs being directly in line with the prints of the front feet, neither too close together nor too far apart. We don't like a horse that "rope walks" (putting one foot over another) behind, or who either dishes or paddles with the front feet. (A horse who is a sluggish mover and who has any irregularities of gait is necessarily handicapped when it comes to going 40, 60, or 100 miles.)

"The next thing we look at are the legs and feet themselves. Is the hoof round and well shaped, the heels wide apart with a good frog and a concave sole? Are the pasterns short and straight or too long and sloping — a moderate slope of about 45 degrees is the best mechanically speaking — and are the pasterns of about medium length? The ankles should be square rather than round; the cannon bones short with the tendons prominent and tightly strung. The knees should be large and flat, while the horse should not be "back at the knee." The forearm should be muscled well but not excessively. Splints are not objectionable if they do not interfere with action of the tendon. As for the hind legs, no curls, jacks, or spavins, no sickle hocks or excessively straight hind legs; the hind leg underneath the horse, rather than trailing behind. Of course, scars, cuts, and bruises indicating that the horse interferes while traveling are a definite handicap.

"As for the body of the horse, a well-coupled horse (a short distance between the last rib and the point of the hip), with a strong loin, will go a lot farther than a loosely coupled horse with a long back. We like an underline that is relatively straight, so as to give plenty of room for the digestive system, not one cut up in the flank or "herring gutted." A good wither to hold the saddle and a good slope of shoulder to take up the jar going downhill are definite advantages. Horses with a deep measurement from the top of the wither to the bottom of the girth, and who are not too wide in the chest, usually have better wind than the round-barreled, wide horse.

"Of course, a horse with a good expression and full eye, the head well set on, the neck reasonably long, set into the top of the shoulders, makes for a more comfortable ride, although many good trail horses get along very well with heads and necks which are something less than the ideal.

"Certainly the general health of the horse is indicated by the amount of flesh he is carrying, and the condition of his coat is also persuasive.

"Of course, some of the horses that are most promising at the preliminary inspection prove to be poor performers on the trail, but generally speaking, the judge gets a pretty good idea ahead of time how the contestants will stack up during the test which lies ahead of them."

Lay judges, unless they have Mr. Mackay-Smith's prestigious reputation, must be certified by the organization to which the Ride belongs. The ECTRA issues a list of approved judges; the Rocky Mountain Conference insists that an experienced horseman sit in at three judgings and assist a veterinarian on at least two Rides before becoming qualified; the NATRC has Horseman Judges and Master Judges. To qualify for the former, a person must be a horseman experienced in Competitive Trail Riding, must serve an apprenticeship during which time he shall be present at two Rides under the supervision of a Master Horseman Judge, shall serve as an assistant on two additional Rides to the Master Horseman Judge, and then judge two Rides independently. After he has received his card, he may be required to pass a written test, and must attend an approved NATRC seminar and judge a Ride during the year.

A lay judge works as hard as a veterinarian, sometimes more so, since he feels he lacks the professional expertise of a veterinarian and is doubly anxious not to make a mistake. This, at least, is my attitude. Having been a competitor and part of the management, I know the effort that has gone into getting the horse to the Ride and staging it, and I want to do my best by both rider and management. This is not as easy as it sounds, since in a few instances, the lay judge and the veterinarian are going to differ, and the lay judge will need facts to back up his arguments.

It is not difficult to be impartial during the Ride and the actual judging, for riders and horses become numbers. Only at the preliminary examination is there time to evaluate the riders as individuals. The veterinarians notice the pretty girls; I study all the competitors, because the horse's performance depends on the person in the saddle. This is not to say that an animal with heart will not finish a Ride even though he has a scarecrow on his back, but he will do much better if his rider assists rather than hinders him.

Usually a sloppily dressed rider has a poorly-cared-for horse. At one of the first Rides I attended, a family of four competed — the parents and a girl and boy with red hair and freckles. They were hard-working farmers who didn't talk much, and slept in the back of a rattly truck. Their saddle blankets were dirty and the horses wormy and cinch-sored. By a miracle, they finished the Ride, but did not place. I thought that was the end of them; it couldn't have been easy to find the entry fee. But they reappeared every year. One time they lost a horse to colic. For a couple of years the judges groaned when they saw the family. I felt sorry for them, knowing it must have been a sacrifice to train the horses when they had the farm work to do, and I felt particularly sorry for the red-headed boy, who tried so hard and so seldom smiled.

At the opposite end of the spectrum was a middle-aged woman who had become an old pro at distance riding. The first Ride she entered, she appeared to be a quiet, mousy person. There were not many competitors and she won a trophy, which caused her to gasp with pleasure. In the en-suing years, she entered every Ride she could. She observed; she learned; she took her horse to California to compete in a fifty-mile Endur-ance Ride, where the real pros showed her how to eliminate competition by deliberately leading her off the trail. Her horse wasn't much to look at. He was an Appy with a big head and a choppy gait, but the woman liked him, and, in a grudging way, the Appy liked her. While the horse never changed, the woman bloomed. She did her hair in a more becom-ing fashion; she wore makeup; and she bought a pair of fancy boots. She became confident, outoing, and one of the most popular competitors on the circuit. When she won a championship, her picture was in the local paper, smiling, with an armful of trophies. She might have stopped there, but she continued riding. She was competitive; she enjoyed win-ning. More important was the all-absorbing, new interest. She was a widow; her children were gone and there was little to do in the small town where she lived.

For a few years, no one seemed able to place a horse above the Appy. Then new riders and new horses began to appear — an Arab stallion, a Morgan, another Appaloosa. At the preliminary check, we judges could see that the new horses were well-conditioned and that their riders were experienced, although the woman did not seem aware that the competi-tion was getting tough.

The veterinarian was aware that the horse was not what he had been. I knew it, too. Our familiarity with the animals could have been an advan-tage or a disadvantage, depending on how one looked at it. The veterinarian treated the local horses, and when those horses appeared in a Ride where he was judging, it was difficult not to evaluate the horse by previous clinical knowledge. While I, a lay judge, was not as informed as a veterinarian, I nevertheless knew a great deal about the horses' per-formances, having observed them on other Rides.

This is a situation that arises in many parts of the country. And, yet, one of the most important lessons a judge can learn is not to make predictions on this basis, a fact that was brought home to me when the new, well-conditioned horses had been winning consistently.

A young woman called me after one of the Rides to protest, "I can't understand why my horse was marked down at the check-in!"

I tried to explain that her horse had not been marked down, but that, in comparison to the top horses, he hadn't shown up well, an explanation which demanded tact.

"Well," the girl said angrily, "if you have to own an Arab or an expensive horse to win, I might as well stop riding."

I could see her point, and it presented a problem. The mediocre animals which had won six or seven years ago were no competition against horses that were a natural for distance riding. They did not need to be Arabs; they could be any breed, but they had to have an extended trot, good legs, lung capacity, and the heart to win.

But what about people who had only one horse they used for hunting and ranch work? Or who had a backyard pet they enjoyed entering in a Ride? What about the beginners on fat ponies, people like the family with the red-haired boy, or the woman with the Appy?

The purpose of distance riding is to promote good horsemanship, and if it becomes too competitive and too professional, it loses its purpose.

The problem was still unsolved at the last Ride of the season, where I was involved in the management and did not know the results of the judging until the awards were made at the dinner. To my surprise, the girl with the nondescript Morgan won the Championship. Afterward, she came over to me, all smiles. "I can't tell you how happy I am! As you know, I was about ready to quit. Now I'm going to keep on, and so are a lot of other people who were getting discouraged, too."

As soon as I found one of the veterinarian judges, I asked him what had happened. "It's simple," he shrugged. "The top horses had been competing all summer and they were lame at the final check."

Such incidents prove that in distance riding, anything can happen. In this case, it was all to the good and our problem was solved.

The horse that I had been sure would win had taken the championship at a Ride where I had been an assistant judge two months before. On this Ride, I had encountered one of the many crises that make judges wish they had taken up Ping-Pong instead of horses. A veterinarian and I were the judges, and the veterinarian chose to go to a checkpoint which could only be reached by jeep and horseback, while I was delegated to the last check on the trail.

"I should be able to join you there," the veterinarian assured me.

The briefing about the trail had not been clear, and I was completely confused after zigzagging on logging roads bulldozed from the side of the Rockies. But this was mild treatment to what I'd been exposed to on other Rides. I had been jounced across mountains in four-wheel-drive vehicles; I'd been lost in the wilderness and pounded to a pulp in the back of a vet's truck as he roared at 70 miles an hour down a dry stream bed.

We reached the check point on time and without incident, followed by two jeep loads of PR teams, timers, and helpers, and parked in a narrow gulch littered with boulders and trapped with bogs.

"Here they come!" someone yelled.

The first riders slid down a steep, timbered trail.

Where was the veterinarian?

To my horror, I saw that the horses were sweating heavily and showed signs of stress they had not shown at the lunch stop. The riding time was fast and the climbs steep. The Competitive Ride had become an Endurance Ride, and since it was the first of the season, the horses were not in the condition they would be in later in the summer.

"Look at this."

An experienced PR boy showed me a high rate penciled on his sheet, at the same time gesturing to the woman with the Appy. To my knowledge, the Appy had never had such high PR's; also, he moved with unaccustomed stiffness.

The confusion was growing in the narrow gulch. More riders were arriving, finding no place to dismount.

Someone caught my arm. "Will you take a look at this black mare? I think she might be tying up."

"Shall I put this horse down as dehydrated?" my recorder asked.

"Can you listen to this heartbeat? It doesn't sound right to me."

"What shall we do about this? Isn't it an inversion?"

In the creek, a rider was sloshing icy water on his hot, sweating animal; the woman with the Appy was taking her own PR's, refusing to believe the official report; a fat girl on a fat pinto was crying. Her horse would have to be pulled. Another girl on an overweight chestnut was angrily loosening her saddle. She, too, would have to be eliminated. Both were new riders and we wanted to encourage them. I tried to explain why I had told them they couldn't continue.

"You don't want to hurt your horse, do you?"

The fat girl sniffled. "But a lady over there told me that my horse's pulse and respiration weren't too high."

"There are other signs of fatigue than PR's," I said.

A rider approached, leading his horse. "Can I go now? I've been rechecked."

There must have been 35 horses in the narrow gulch along with the jeeps, trucks, riders and helpers. As I stepped back to avoid being trampled by a big roan, I tried to tell myself to remain calm, as the Veterinary Handbook advised. Be very sure, very firm. Don't make decisions hastily. Fatigue shouldn't be confused with exhaustion. A horse that has gone fifty miles might look tired, but can go on with no ill effects (Dr. Bruce Bascomb); evaluate by prolonged capillary refill time, cyanotic mucous membranes. The trouble was that there wasn't time to do all this thoroughly. Right or wrong, I decided on one thing — a pulse of 70 or over would mean the horse would be held and rechecked in fifteen minutes. If the pulse didn't go down, the horse would be eliminated. That was the criterion on Endurance Rides. It was better to err on the side of caution than to be permissive and lose or injure a horse. Also, some decisions were made on the basis of the riders — would they take it easy the rest of the way if I asked them to?

Somehow, with the help of the efficient PR crews and timers, we got the last rider checked out. Thankfully, none failed to arrive at the finish line, where I found the veterinarian talking to the woman who owned the Appy.

The veterinarian was saying, "I'm afraid he has arthritis. You notice he isn't moving the way he used to."

The woman stroked the ugly old head. "I guess I know it, but I hate to admit it. I don't know how I'll keep on riding without him."

When the woman had led the Appy away, the veterinarian shook his head. He was a nice young man. "Gee, I hated to tell her that. Say, how did you get along at the checkpoint?"

"I survived," I said. "What happened to you?"

The veterinarian grinned. "Oh, I got stuck on the top of the mountain."

This does not mean that crises are a common occurrence on distance Rides. A judge may attend any number of Rides and experience only routine, but there is always an exception, such as the Competitive turned Endurance Ride, and a Ride the year before when I, as lay judge, was called on to render a decision that would have taxed Solomon. As unofficial representatives of the conference or association, lay judges are frequently appealed to by the management.

This Ride was well organized, with accommodations in a grassy fairground adjoining a river. Many riders had entered because the conference donated a handsome buckle to those who completed four Rides out of all the Rides in the conference. Included in the entries was the family with the red-headed boy. Again, a veterinarian and I were the judges. At the briefing, the trail boss explained the route the competitors would take the following day. He did not have the customary map, but felt it was not necessary.

"You can't get lost," he explained. "If you get off the trail, all you got to do is go downhill."

He pointed to a range of mountains looming 9000 feet above the valley. "A' course, you might see a rattlesnake or two, and there's bears around."

All went well for the first check and the noon stop. At the last check before the finish, we waited by the side of a logging road. The veterinarian, the Ride manager, the trail boss, the PR crews, and the timers waited with us.

"Here comes someone!" the trail boss cried.

It was the red-headed boy on his quarter horse, accompanied by his father.

"Where are the others?" the veterinarian asked.

The boy shook his head. "I dunno. I ain't seen them."

As usual, his freckled face was serious.

The boy had a fifteen-minute check and continued toward the fairgrounds, but his father's horse was eliminated for lameness. I did notice, however, that the horse was better taken care of than it had been formerly, and that the blanket and cinch were clean.

We waited and waited. Still no riders.

Finally the chairman and the trail boss drove off to look for them. At the end of another half hour, it was decided that I would return to the fairgrounds, while the veterinarian waited at the checkpoint.

Hours later, the riders appeared, all of them eliminated on time. They'd taken a wrong turning and lost their way.

"What'll we do?" the chairman asked.

The riders were equally upset. The trail had been steep and rocky, and they were tired.

"We feel like giving up for the summer," they told me. "We'd planned on this Ride to make one of the four for the buckle. If we can't count it, we can't compete for the buckle. There's only one other Ride left, and that's at Jackson, which is too far for us to go."

I might have told the riders it was their own fault, but I hadn't seen the trail. Perhaps it had not been as well marked as it should have been. And also, the riders were genuinely discouraged, which concerned me. Many of them had supported our Conference for years, and had done more than their share to make distance riding in our area a success. Were the rules to be abided by under all circumstances, or could they be changed if the situation warranted?

I located a telephone booth by a motel on the highway and called the co-chairman of the conference. The conversation, long distance and with trucks roaring by, was difficult, but eventually we reached a solution that proved acceptable to the Ride Chairman.

The following morning at the awards gathering, I stood up. "I'm afraid that those who failed to finish on time are ineligible for trophies or ribbons on the Ride. Nor can you count the Ride for the buckle."

Glum silence greeted the information.

"However," I added, "instead of four Rides to qualify for the buckle, you will now need to complete only three."

Clapping and cheers. That crisis was solved.

But the climax was yet to come. When I sat down, the chairman stood up. "There are no places in the heavyweight or lightweight divisions, but in the junior division, we have first place — "

The red-headed boy stepped forward as his name was called.

"The best-conditioned horse!"

Again the boy got up.

"Best Quarter Horse!"

"Grand champion!"

When it was over, the red-headed boy had an armful of silver, a saddle blanket, a rhinestone-studded halter, and a bridle.

Still, he never smiled. He was afraid to; if he had, he might have cried.

18. The Management: The Rewards Are Not Monetary

THE MANAGEMENT is loosely defined as the people who put on a Ride, and includes officials who have various titles in different parts of the country, but who perform the same duties. Sometimes the authority is vested solely in these officials, and sometimes in a board of stewards (Virginia 100-Mile in Three Days Ride) or a board of directors (Florida). The management can consist of individuals drawn together by a common interest, or members of a saddle club or breed organization. For instance, the Florida Horsemen's Association backs the Florida 100-Mile in Three Days Ride, and their Board of Directors appoints the Ride officials. This is also true of the Green Mountain Horse Association, which is responsible for the 100-Mile Competitive Ride at South Woodstock, Vermont.

Numerous volunteers assist at the Ride, but the officials are busy all year. Indeed, the symbol of Trail Ride management should be hard work, so that before a Ride is scheduled, people would know how much time they can devote to the project, and their degree of interest. It also helps to have ingenuity, patience, Trail Ride experience, and the knowledge that while the judges and contestants are responsible for a segment of the event, the management is responsible for everything.

Financial profit is denied them. Indeed, a Ride is fortunate to meet expenses. Many, like the Bitterroot, incorporate as nonprofit, although there are other reasons for incorporation than the desire to show impoverishment; the main reason is to escape the amusement tax levied on ventures that charge entry fees.

The first problem facing the management is where to have the Ride. Happily, there are areas nearly everywhere in the United States suitable for trails. The officials might be familiar with the area, and if they are not, they might take an exploratory tour on horseback, and then find a good detailed map. Is the land privately owned? Forest Service land?

Bureau of Land Management? State property? Before further plans are made, permission should be secured from the various agencies or individuals concerned, and the trail can then be measured by jeep and by odometer where there is no road. When we measured the trail for the Bitterroot Ride, my husband tied a long pole onto the handle of the odometer and pushed it ahead of him on horseback, which was easier than walking.

At this time, the mileage is determined — 40 miles, or 35, or if the Ride is a one-day Endurance Ride, 50 miles.

Other decisions to be made are whether to stage a one-, two-, or three-day event; and if a novice Ride is to be held in conjunction with the regular Ride; and how long it will be and on what part of the trail.

Sheer walls of rock, bogs, slides, and other perilous obstacles should be avoided. Downed timber should be cleared from the trail and holes filled with earth. To some people, these hazards might be unimportant, or add zest to the competition, but it is well to remember that if a contestant is injured, not only does the Ride suffer a bad name, but a suit for damages might result.

Once the trail is measured, it has to be marked with arrows painted on rocks, blazes on trees, ribbons tied to branches, or paper plates nailed to whatever is possible. Unfortunately, on one Ride cattle ate the paper plates, and sometimes the Forest Service, bent on business of its own, ties ribbons to branches too, which creates confusion, but is only one of the many exigencies with which the management has to deal. This is why it is advisable, a day or so before the Ride, to see if the markers are still visible. It is also a good idea to send a stranger over the trail. If he can find his way, the marking is successful; if he can't, the trail should be re-marked.

A touch of humor helps; my husband paints features on snags and rocks which resemble animals, while at Jackson Hole, Wyoming, riders encountered bones by the trail labeled, "One Who Didn't Make It!"

As soon as the trail is finished, it should be ridden at Endurance or Competitive Ride speed to determine the riding time, which could be 6½ to 7 hours for 40 miles on a Competitive Ride to 4½ hours for a 50 mile Endurance Ride.

Where are the checkpoints to be? The veterinarians prefer them to be at the tops of steep climbs. And what about the noon lunch stop, which must have an area large enough for spectators, helpers, the food van, and numerous vehicles? Like all stops, it must be accessible by truck or jeep.

Plans should be made for trailers to be in strategic locations in case a horse has to be hauled out. And water must be available at the noon stop and on the trail.

When a fairground is near the Ride area, get in touch with the County Commissioners to ask if the facilities are available. If no fairground is close by, other arrangements will have to be made with private stables or with National or State Parks or the Forest Service.

While the trail is being measured, volunteers should be enlisted. Many of them will have nothing to do until the day of the Ride, six months away; others might need some training, such as members of the PR teams if they have not served in that capacity before. But the success of the Ride depends on the unpaid helpers, whatever their duties. Clinics are a good way to stir up interest in the beginning. The local veterinarian or representative from a national breed association, or one of the Ride organizations, might give a talk and show a film. From the interested people who attend these meetings, there should be selected a publicity chairman, a chairman for the PR teams, one for the timers and recorders, a stable manager, a person to collect trophy donations, a chairman for the safety riders, a food chairman and a night watchman.

On the Florida Ride, the Chairman is called a Superintendent, and it is his duty to see that the Ride operates efficiently, to receive complaints, and to act as intermediary between the judges and the riders. On NATRC events, the Chairman is supposed to be an experienced horseman and a capable executive, and is entrusted (according to the management manual) with 34 responsibilities, among which are holding meetings to keep personnel informed of the Ride's progress and to hear committee reports, obtaining the contestants' numbers, and arranging for the judges. That may sound intimidating to a new management, and yet putting on a Ride should be a pleasure, not a chore. Much depends on the attitude of the chairman, which is reflected by the others. When the volunteers are made to feel part of the organization and know that their suggestions are listened to, they will tackle their jobs with enthusiasm.

On the Bitterroot Ride, we add an extra touch—volunteer hostesses who greet the contestants and serve free coffee and cookies. If a rider is a stranger, he is made to feel welcome and becomes a member of the group. A contestant who is ignored is apt to become discouraged and not return the following year.

The next question is: should the Ride be sanctioned by the NATRC, the Rocky Mountain Conference, the ECTRA, the American Endurance Ride Conference, or a similar organization?

If sanctioned, a Ride must abide by the organization's rules, which may not always be acceptable, and a membership fee can add to the cost. But on the whole, the benefits outweigh the disadvantages.

Once a Ride is sanctioned, a date is set which will not conflict with other Rides, and which, it is hoped, will not be on the same day as the local fair or horse show. The organizations furnish material on how to start a Ride and some will send a representative to explain to the officials the procedures to be followed. The organizations will also furnish lists of riders and other Rides, while members become eligible for a conference high-point trophy and buckle. The NATRC has membership dues for individuals and families, and the Ride pays the organization a fee. In return, the NATRC provides judges' sheets, insurance at a moderate rate, and names of approved judges, and includes the Ride on its official schedule.

However, most of the publicity must be done by the local management, such as placing the Ride dates in the coming-events columns of magazines and sending notices to the local papers, television, and radio stations. Entry blanks should be mailed to prospective riders.

The entry blanks should be published three to six months ahead, and should contain as much pertinent information as space permits. A good example of a one-page entry blank is sent out by the Vermont 100-Mile Ride, on which there are spaces for the horse's name, sex, age, height, breed, name of sire, and name of dam. (These last two questions are asked by few Rides.) Also requested are the name of the rider, and such information as — have you ridden in the Green Mountain Horse Association 100-Mile Ride? How many years have you ridden? Other riding experience, such as hunting, showing or polo? Have you owned horses and had experience with their care in stables and on trails?

Again, the request for personal information is not customarily seen on entry blanks, but it might be considered by managements, for it is a source of valuable data. The horse and rider are a team and something should be known about the rider as well as his mount.

Entry fees and stable fees are also shown on the entry blank, and on the bottom of the page, a space is reserved for the contestant's signature below the statement that there will be no refund of entry fee for cancellation later than thirty days before the start of the Ride. This part of the blank may be cut off and mailed back to the Green Mountain Horse Association with a check or money order.

Refunds are a problem, and at an early date it should be determined within what period before the Ride refunds will be made, and if a five or ten dollar penalty will be charged to cover costs. This should be on the entry blank.

Also included should be a notice that a Coggins test and a certificate of soundness is required, if the Ride demands it.

Some entry blanks, like the Old Dominion 100-Mile Endurance Ride at Leesburg, Virginia, are veritable manuals on distance riding. They are published on heavy-duty stock and include not only a map of the trail, the entry fee, accommodations, the Ride schedule, list of trophies, and the rules, but also an article entitled, "Some Thoughts on Endurance Riding." Photographs show the previous year's winners.

This is an excellent booklet, to be kept in a rider's equestrian library, but it is too expensive for most Rides to publish and mail.

In addition, entry blanks may carry information about motels, camping, and meals. The NATRC Rides charge for meals; the Bitterroot Ride offers a free awards banquet, free lunch on the trail, and free breakfasts. The Vermont Ride fee, higher than average, covers the rider's lunches on two days, the breakfast lunches, a banquet on the first evening, and a final awards supper on the last night. The Tevis provides no meals or accommodations, nor do many Endurance events; as can be seen, there is no general rule in this respect, which makes it desirable to print the information on the entry brochure for the rider who is on a budget and must estimate his expenses. So far, no Ride is so expensive that cost is a determining factor in whether or not a rider will enter. Cost *is* a factor to the managements, whose expenses are considerable and whose income is limited to entry fees and donations from business firms. If the management offers too many free meals, it will either have to raise the entry fee or operate at a deficit.

As the day of the Ride approches, tension mounts. Will there be too many riders? Or not enough? Do all the members of the PR teams have stethoscopes? Is it going to rain? Is that steep place on the trail before the lunch stop too dangerous? What if a rider is hurt? Or a horse injured?

The Old Dominion brochure contains this statement: "It is impossible to anticipate problems or circumstances which may arise during the course of the ride event."

Sensible advice, and yet the management continues to be torn between apprehension and expectation. In my case, edginess is magnified by fatigue, for the officials get little sleep, nor does anyone else for that matter. The riders are up late and early, caring for their horses; the helpers tending to their duties; and the officials dealing with the "circumstances that arise."

The day before the Ride, the Secretary, who is the hardest working and most capable official, checks in the contestants. At the Bitterroot Ride, the office is a large trailer parked in the fairgrounds. Each contestant is given an envelope with a name tag, number, map, information sheet, and a card for his stall. His name is checked off on a master list and his judge's card given to the head recorder. He is then weighed, unless he is a junior or a novice, and assigned his stall.

We also have a 20-mile Ride in conjunction with the two-day Ride to encourage new riders who lack experience, or whose horses are not sufficiently conditioned for 60 miles. The Virginia 100-Mile Ride has a 50-Mile in Three Days Ride for the same reason, and many NATRC events hold novice Rides, which a beginner would be wise to enter before attempting a longer distance. The trouble is that two Rides complicate matters for the management. The Secretary has two separate sets of entries; the time schedules must be arranged so that the 60-milers do not get tangled up with the 20-milers on the trail; a separate judge, recorders, and PR crews must be assigned the 20-mile, and arrangements made for the novices to check in while the Bitterroot Ride contestants are doing the forty miles the first day. This is because the novices do the same twenty miles as the others on the second day, only they start fifteen minutes later.

All this is planned to the split second by the capable co-chairman, my friend, Margit, and her assistants, but I can't help thinking, what if—.

Trucks and trailers are rolling into the fairgrounds; riders are unloading horses and leading them around; PR girls are taking pulse and respiration on haltered animals held by their owners; spectators are inspecting the trophies displayed on a table by the hostess's house, and watching the preliminary examinations by the veterinarians and wondering what it is all about. The drag riders are looking for the radios; the photographer is snapping pictures.

Thankfully, the sun shines. Sometimes it doesn't — it snows or rains — or it is stifling hot, and then the management has a crisis.

In the trailer, the secretary is copying lists of contestants for the judges, and at the same time is telling a man where he can telephone to find out why his horses, which were in a truck behind him, have not arrived. Over the loudspeaker, the announcer is calling, "No. 6. The judges are waiting!"

Each rider has been given a number which tells him approximately when he will be called for the preliminary check, which eliminates the tiresome periods of waiting (another suggestion by our volunteers, and one that has proved beneficial).

The preliminary examination always takes longer than estimated, which means there is little time for the judges and contestants to eat before the briefing, which is held on the grass near the hostess's house (if it isn't raining). A volunteer who has become an invaluable addition to the Ride has hooked up a public address system to his truck so that the trail boss can explain the trail, the officials the rules, and the veterinarians what they will be looking for. Veterinarians are usually not articulate before a microphone, so the briefing is not long.

Starting time for the forty miles is seven o'clock; breakfast is from five to six o'clock, cooked by members of a local Grange in one of the fair buildings. Some years, the Chamber of Commerce provides a free breakfast, for the Ride has excellent support from the local businessmen, an important factor in making any Ride a success. At five o'clock it is chilly and barely light, but as the announcer calls the numbers of the riders who are waiting on the starting line at seven o'clock, the sun comes up. The riders go out at 15-second intervals, trotting through the flag-festooned gate and across the meadows still in shadow, although the sun is bright on the mountains. As the last rider departs, the judges, timers, PR crews, and recorders dash for the trucks and jeeps. One of the most important duties of the co-chairman has been to arrange transportation for the necessary officials, as well as the operating procedures. Each judge knows where he is to go; the drag riders are already on the trail, equipped with radios; the spotters, who remain stationary and check the riders as they go by, have been in place for some time; trailers have been parked at strategic places, in case a horse has to be hauled back to the fairgrounds.

Happily, no "circumstances" arise. I do not get to the checkpoints, but I do get to the lunch stop, where the food is catered by a local restaurant owner — sandwiches, fruit, coffee, and punch. The portable rest rooms are set up among the trees and the water truck is parked in a place that is convenient for the riders to reach with their buckets. Some Rides do not permit helpers, but we allow one to each contestant. Also, the one-hour lunch stop is taken out of the riding time.

As the riders appear on the trail, they are noted by the timers, then directed by a traffic controller to a PR team, who takes the horse's pulse and respiration before passing him on to a veterinarian. At the end of fifteen minutes, the horses are checked again. After that, the riders are free to do what they want for the remainder of the hour. Some sponge their horses' legs; some stretch out in the shade of a pine tree; others gather around the lunch wagon. The chairmen stand in the background and watch, which is proper, for a Ride should be so well organized that it runs automatically. But if "circumstances" arise the management is present to deal with the emergency.

That evening there is a briefing for the 20-milers. While it is going on, the PR teams and recorders copy their notes for the day onto master forms which will be referred to by the judges during the final evaluation. On each form is stapled a Polaroid picture of the horse taken at the preliminary check, so that if the judge forgets a horse, he can refresh his memory by glancing at the picture. This is an innovation of the Bitterroot Trail Ride that the management, through experience, has found helpful.

In the morning, the 60-milers go out at seven, the 20-milers fifteen minutes later. Riding time for the first group is 2 to 2½ hours, and for the 20-milers, 3½ to 4 hours. This means that Margit and I can drive to the 15-minute check point, the only one on the trail that day, and get back to the fairgrounds before the Sixty Milers start coming in. The number of novices worries us, for the risk of injury is greater than with experienced riders. At the checkpoint, a hollow among sage-covered hills where a spring bubbles into a stock tank, the judge and his crew are checking contestants. It is threatening rain and I glance anxiously at the sky. If the weather remains favorable, half of the managements' problems cease to exist.

The number of riders dwindles. The recorder checks her lists, says something to the veterinarian, and walks over to us. Number 26 is missing.

"Who is 26?"

We refer to our list and discover that 26 is a young girl who has never ridden in a Trail Ride before, and who has a reputation for being timid.

"We're sure we checked her out this morning," the recorder says.

Unhooking the radio from the dashboard of the jeep, Margit says, "I'll try to get the drag riders . . . Calling Number 8! Calling number 8!"

When a reply sputters over the radio, Margit said, "Have you seen number 26?"

"No rider with that number has passed here."

Replacing the radio, Margit gets into the jeep; I follow. "We'll go back over the trail. Perhaps a spotter or drag rider will have seen the girl. If not, we'll have to return to the fairgrounds and organize a search crew.''

In the jeep we jolt over sagebrush that fell away to green valley laced with a river and fringed with cottonwoods. On the west rise the grey stone peaks that form the Idaho-Montana border. Is that something moving beyond the clump of pines? Is that a horse coming up out of the draw? No, it's only a cow.

At a parked truck, Margit puts on the brakes. "We're missing a rider. Have you seen a girl on a horse? Number 26?''

The man sitting at the wheel refers to his list and shakes his head. "No one with that number has come by here, and I've seen 'em all.''

The man's reply increases our concern. "We'll have to go back to the fairgrounds,'' Margit decided.

As we race toward the fairgrounds trailing dust, we discuss the plan that would be instituted for the emergency. Swinging through the gate, Margit squeals to a halt before the office. As we leap out of the car, the Secretary appears at the door of the trailer, shouting and waving her arms.

"Wait! Wait! Marvin radioed in that you were missing a rider. She just appeared. She overslept and never started. The veterinarian must have made a mistake when he thought he checked her out.''

Both Margit and I breathe, "Thank God!'' Of all the crises that can occur, the management fears a lost rider more than anything else.

By this time, the Sixty Milers are coming in. As they ride through the gate where the flags still flutter, the announcer calls their numbers and tells something about each rider, which makes an otherwise unspectacular finish interesting to the spectators. Trail Rides are not as exciting to watch as a jumping event or a rodeo; a person must be a knowledgeable horseman or related to one of the contestants to stand for an hour to watch a bunch of horses come walking in. On the Bitterroot Ride, we feel that the spectators should be encouraged, for they give support to distance riding, and from their ranks we draw future contestants.

The horses are checked in as soon as they cross the finish line, and after one hour are checked again, following which the judges retire to the house to make final evaluations. The management can sit in at the judging, but does not make critical comments or try to influence the decisions in any respect. The placings are entirely up to the judges.

Usually the placings are not decided until the guests are arriving for the awards dinner, which is served buffet style beneath the cottonwood trees in the stable area of the Bitterroot Stock Farm. Nearly 300 people gather at tables covered with red and white checkered cloths, eating chicken, barbecued ribs, fruit salad, potato salad, corn on the cob, rolls, cake, and pie. Young people, old people, children, riders, businessmen. After the dinner, the awards are presented. The riders are called by name and number, starting with Number 6 in each division and working up to the climax of the Grand Champion. By this time the lights hung among the trees have been turned on. Riders step up, receive a buckle or ribbon or trophy with a smile, and step back. The Champion poses with a large silver cup and streamers of purple ribbons.

The applause subsides and the crowd thins. At last it's over! We can relax and sleep as we haven't been able to do for weeks. I feel as though I never want to be part of the management again; this is the last Trail Ride!

People come up to say good-bye and thank Margit for the dinner.

"Next year," a rider says.

"Next year — ," a PR girl tells us.

"Next year," a veterinarian judge declares.

We smile back, forgetting how tired we are. Next year? Why, of course, there will be another Ride. In our preoccupation with our work we have failed to realize that the management, too, receives its awards. We are appreciated by people; we have enjoyed it. With the riders and volunteers, we form a team that has accomplished our purpose of encouraging the raising, riding, and conditioning of horses, regardless of breed or price. We have not made a financial profit, but no amount of money could buy the knowledge that we have acquired, the days on the trail, and the comradeship.

That is what makes distance riding worthwhile.

APPENDIX
BIBLIOGRAPHY
INDEX

Number	Division	Prelim.	1ˢᵗ Day – 40 miles										2ⁿ Day – 20 miles										
			1ˢᵗ Check		2ˢᵗ Check		Noon		Finish				1ˢᵗ Check		2ˢᵗ Check		Finish						
			in	out	in	out	in	out	in.	I hr.			in	out	in	out	in	I hr					
Temperature.																							
Pulse																							
Respiration																							

Soundness. (45%)	Score.

Condition (45%)	

Suitability ◊ General Attitude (10%)	

Horsemanship (Junior)	Score -	Time.
		40 miles Hr. Min.
	Place -	20 " ___ " ___ "
		60 " ___ " ___ "
		Penalty Points —

Rider's Name.	Adress.	Other Awards.	Total Score —
Horse Name.	Age / Sex	Weight / Height.	Breed / Color		Place —

JUDGE'S SHEET

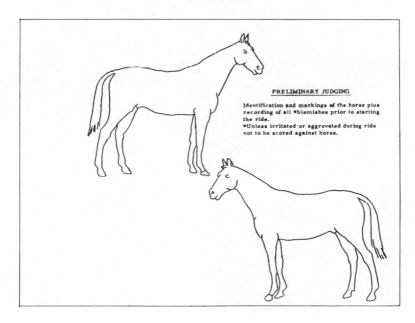

PRELIMINARY JUDGING

Identification and markings of the horse plus recording of all *blemishes prior to starting the ride.
*Unless irritated or aggrevated during ride not to be scored against horse.

| PRELIMINARY CHECK - | | | | | | FIRST CHECK | | | | | -20 MILES FINAL CHECK | | | | | | |
Horse No.	Temp.	Pulse	Resp.	Comments	Horse No.	Pulse In	Pulse Out	Resp In	Resp Out	Time	Pulse In	Pulse 1 Hr	Resp In	Resp 1. Hr.	Temp.	TIME	Comments

FORM FOR PULSE AND RESPIRATION

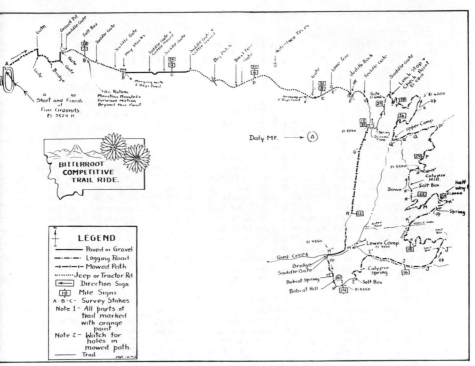

EXAMPLE OF TRAIL RIDE MAP

BITTERROOT
COMPETITIVE
TRAIL RIDE.

BITTERROOT

1st Day - 40 miles - 6½ to 7 hour[s]

Place	Name	Number	State	Horse	Breed	Sex	Age	Weight	Height	Friday Check T.P.R.	10 mile Check Pulse·Resp. In-Out In-Out	18 mile Check Pulse·Resp. In-Out In-Out	28½ Miles (noon) Pulse·Resp. Temp. In-Out In-Out	Com

Junior Division.

1st	Brian Wood	1	Ida.	Smokey	QH	G	6	950	14² 99.4	44	12	76-62 28-12	84-68 52-28	101⁸ 68-52 36-12	
2nd	Patricia McDonald	13	Mont.	Laddy	A/TB	6	5	950	15 100⁺	40	36	96-80 116-64	80-64 92-40	102² 72-64 84-40	
3rd	Karyn Cozad	11	Mont.	Paco Tibo	Ap	G	8	1050	14² 100⁴	44	30	72-56 92-36	76-64 80-68	100⁹ 76-60 44-48	
4th	Donna Walker	14	Mont.	Coalie	QH/TB	G	8	1150	16 100	40	12	72-64 76-56	92-60 72-60	101⁹ 96-44 60-24	
5th	Susan Reilly	10	Cal.	Medicine Hat	mst	M	10	1000	14² 100!	44	28	80-60 100-52	72-60 64-48	101⁵ 76-60 104-20	
6th	Susanne Hayes	5	Mont.	Ajax	TB/G	7	1200	17 100⁴	36	21	60-48 100-48	72-56 108-68	101⁵ 72-48 76-20	
	Justin Cozad	2	Mont.	Sir Patches	Ap	G	6	1200	16 99²	40	16	68-52 72-28	84-68 88-40	100⁶ 80-48 88-40	
	Mary Pat Sias	3	Mont.	Duchie	Mor	M	6	1000	15² 100⁺	60	24	88-64 108-48	72-56 92-52	101⁸ 72-52 60-16	
	Katheryn McDonald	4	Mont.	Valentine	Mor TB	M	8	1075	15 100⁺	76	24	88-98 104-60	78-56 100-56		
	Pat Gilmore	6	Mont.	Rock Cinch	QH	G	11	1150	15 99²	40	20	128 136	96-76 160-120	Held ten minutes - E[limin]	
	Vicki Johnson	7	Mont.	Lady	QH	M	6	900	14.! 100⁺	40	26	64 64-68-56	84-56 92-40	99² 88-52 72-32	Elim
	Jeff Soest	8	Wyo.	Buddy	QH	G	6	1000	14² 101	44	44	116-68 136-40	96-68 76-64	102²-104-52 108-36	
	Virginia Rasmussen	9	Mont.	My Lady Pirate	QH	M	6	900	13² 99⁸	44	40	76-64 76-48	92-60 76-40		Elim

Lightweight Division.

1st	Ickell Moore	25	Mont.	Skookum Parchico	Ap	G	9	1050	15²100⁵	42	32	76-64 72-28	80-68 88-52	100⁹ 76-44 104-24	
2nd	Charmaine Roberts	30	Ida.	Talote	A/Mor	G	9	1050	15² 99.6	40	20	89-56 60-28	64-48 80-28	101⁹ 76-40 68-24	
3rd	Susanna Anderson	27	Mont.	Bolenas Joe	QH	G	9	950	14.2 98.²	40	24	76-52 88-32	80-64 56-24	102⁴ 88-60 52-16	
4th	Tex Johnson	22	Mont.	Voodoo M'Coo	Ap	M	9	1100	15 100⁺	44	20	76-56 60-20	80-60 96-44	100⁹ 60-52 64-28	
5th	Lindy Duus	20	Mont.	Duus Cinders	Ap	M	7	1000	14² 100⁺	44	28	88-60 132-60	92-76 112-80	101⁵ 84-60 92-28	
6th	Althea C. Soest	23	Wyo.	Gypsy	QH	M	7	1100	14² 100!	40	40	80-68 112-72	120-60 112-80	100⁹ 88-52 68-36	
	Esther McDonald	21	Mont.	Spooky	QH	M	8	1050	15²100!	16	40	112-72 116-80	92-76 76-40	102²-104-60 76-12	
	Glenda Reynolds	24	Mont.	Dan	18	G	13	1150	16⁵ 100	40	32	80-56 104-72	96-64 92-80	101⁸ 96-60 80-18	
	Linda Satterfield	26	Wyo.	LaVernis Dandy	Ap	G	6	1000	15² 100!	44	20	76-56 68-88	68-48 96-48	102² 88-44 76-48	
	Eleanor Victor	28	Mont.	Lica Rose	QH	M	7	1250	15² 100!	40	28	72-56 88-24	88-64 68-72	100⁺ 112-52 76-24	
	Barbara Rupe	29	Cal.	Sundown	QH	M	5	1100	14² 100⁺	36	24	88-64 124-92	80-64 124-72	102⁵ 80-48 112-44	
	Lynn Taylor	31	Mont.	Skipjack	Ap	G	7	1000	14²100!	44	20	72-60 84-52	80-64 108-76	100⁵ 72-48 100-36	

Heavyweight Division.

1st	Carl Koenen	75	Ida.	Kortina Ace	Arab	M	7	1000	14² 100⁸	40	44	104 40 72 68	100-72 64 60	102² 96 56 64 16	
2nd	Kelly Robbins	77	Mont.	Copper	QH TB	G	11	1125	15² 100!	44	28	108 68 84 60	92-64 64 28	88 48 60 16	
3rd	Thelma Fitzgerald	60	Mont.	Big Red	A/TB	G	10	1150	15² 98⁸	44	24	80 60 84 72	80-60 92 48	80 44 100 28	
4th	Jim Rains	69	Wyo.	Penny	Gr	M	12	1050	15² 100⁺	40	36	96-56 68 80	88-60 104-92	100⁺ 104 48 64 52	
5th	Shirley Lane	63	Mont.	New Yorker	TB	G	10	1100	15² 100⁺	44	28	84-56 100 68	68 56 100 68	100⁹ 76-48 76-16	
6th	Clifford Trollope	61	Mont.	Golda Boy	TB/A	G	5	1100	16 101⁸	48	32	72-56 72-52	68-52 108-64	101⁵ 72-56 52-36	
	Connie Kerr	51	Mont.	Buck	Gr	G	7	1000	15² 100!	40	32	100-52 104-80	Lost trail - Eliminated.		
	Tessa Bradt	64	Mont.	John Ash	Mor	G	9	975	14² 100!	44	28	100-72 104-52	104-68 72-60	102⁵ 96-72 108-24	
	Betty DuPont	65	Mont.	Osaye Torrette	QH	M	8	1200	14² 100⁸	40	16	64-48 64-28	92-76 76-32	Rider withdrew	
	Dan Leonardi	67	Mont.	Poco	TB	G	8	1250	15² 100!	36	20	80-64 60-60	96-68 104-64	102² 76-52 92-20	
	Trudie Lyons	68	Can.	Bill	TB/QH	G	6	1200	15²		52-28	88-72 104-60	84-64 64-60	102² 84-60 76-44	
	Orin Soest	70	Wyo.	Teton Romeo	Mor	G	5	1000	14² 100⁺	44	28	88-56 120-60	76-60 80-28	101⁵ 80-68 108-32	
	Ann Hayes	71	Mont.	Kootenai Janus	Mor	G	5	1000	15² 100⁺	56	28	72-52 68-52	76-60 80-28	100² 100-60 80-28	
	Clare Johnson	72	Mont.	Raini Rumels	QH	G	8	1100	16² 100⁺	44	20	68-48 72-32	72 88		Elim
	Barbara Clark	73	Wyo.	Miss Fall Breeze	QH	M	6	1150	15² 100⁴	40	28	64-48 68-64	64-52 116-108	100⁹ 78-52 108-56	
	Marc Fischer	74	Wyo.	Khamelot	Ar.	G	9	1150	15² 100	40	44	76-56 76-64	80-60 120-80	101⁵ 60-48 72-40	
	Kavyn Hamilton	76	Mont.	Dusk	QH	M	7	1000	14² 100⁺	68	56	Eliminated because of high temp + l[ameness]			

EXAMPLE OF TRAIL RIDE CHART SENT OUT TO CONTESTANTS

COMPETITIVE TRAIL RIDE

HAMILTON,
MONTANA.
Aug. 19, 20, 21, 1970.

2ⁿᵈ Day – 20 miles – 2½ to 3 hours.

Total Trail Miles	Temp. Pulse Resp. In-1hr. In-1hr. 1a-1hr	Comments.	Time 10mile 2.0 Pulse Resp miles In-Out In-Out	No.	20 miles Finish –1hr. Pulse. Resp. Temp. In-Out 1a-Out	Time Penalty	T.P.R 100 pts	Cond. Sound ness 75 pts.	Fatigue 100 pts.	Main crs 26 pts	Total Points 300
7:01	101.6 68-60 32-28		2:44 64-48 32-12	1	101.1 60-36 20-8		86	56	86	25	253
6:52	72-60 44-36		2:38 80-60 74-48	13	101.3 64-56 60-16		80	69	80	19	248
6:58	102² 92-61 92-44		2:40 72-60 88-56	11	99⁵ 68-48 60-28		76	58	90	23	247
6:40	101¹ 88-40 88-40		2:57 84-64 100-88	14	101⁸ 72-48 64-24		78	60	82	25	245
6:50	102¹ 88-56 104-24		2:55 80-72 80-44	10	101³ 64-52 40-12		82	57	78	25	242
6:59	102² 68-52 68-24		2:53 60-48 80-28	5	100⁶ 52-48 40-20		84	58	74	24	240
6:57	104/₄₂ 88-48 88-36		2:45 80-72 100-48	2	101⁶ 52-48 96-24	–	74	54	86	25	239
8:11	101.3 64-56 64-28	Disqualified because of Time.		3		–					
				4							
...ated.				6							
...d.				7							
6:48	101² 88-44 60-24	Novice Rider.		8							
...d.				9							
6:43	98² 80-48 104-20		2:51 76-60 108-52	25	99⁴ 68-52 60-20		84	60	86	25	255
6:45	102 80-52 76-20		2:46 80-64 84-50	30	101⁸ 68-36 68-16		90	56	83	25	254
7:08	100⁹ 96-52 72-44	8 Penalty Points	2:55 76-52 64-36	27	100² 68-44 52-12	–8	86	61	86	25	250
6:48	102⁰ 52-60 48-24		2:50 84-56 80-44	22	99⁶ 52-52 52-26		77	61	86	25	249
6:57	103³ 100-60 88-40		2:53 76-64 120-40	20	101⁴ 60-44 100-12		82	56	84	25	247
6:43	102³ 88-48 140-20		2:38 104-60 86-80	23	101⁶ 80-60 104-20		73	61	84	25	243
6:51	80-60 52-36		2:46 100-80 84-64	21	103³ 96-68 44-28		71	69	82	10	232
6:50	101.6 84-56 84-44		2:49 84-68 120 84	24	101¹ 84-98 80-32		75	61	78	25	239
6:54	101⁸ 80-48 108-28		2:55 68-48 92-48	26	101 64-44 48-16		88	61	68	25	242
7:08	103/₁₀₀ 96-60 140-44	8 Penalty Points	2:44 92-54 92-12	28	100⁶ 72-48 68-24	–8	80	48	84	25	229
6:40	101/₁₀₀ 84-44 112-28		2:35 96-64 92-20	29	103⁵/₁₀₀ 72-76 108-48		70	58	76	25	229
6:43	101⁶ 84-44 112-56		2:40 84-54 104-72	31	100⁶ 68-48 84-36		79	59	76	23	237
6:51	102³/₄₄ 72-72 60-32		2:51 92-76 100-64	75	102⁴ 88-60 56-24		81	67	86	25	259
6:57	101³ 64-52 40-36		2:47 96-60 88-52	77	100⁴ 68-48 60-24		87	58	84	25	254
6:45	102³ 68-40 80-40		2:40 80-60 84-100	60	102⁸ 76-44 112-12		85	63	80	23	251
6:48	103³ 80-52 96-36		2:53 84-60 100-100	69	101⁸ 72-44 112-40		75	61	88	25	249
6:54	101³ 88-48 120-36		2:52 68-48 96-32	63	101⁶ 68-44 64-20		87	55	78	25	245
6:50	104³/₁₀₁ 88-44 132-24		2:52 80-72 84-92	61	102³ 84-56 128-20		83	70	86	25	244
				51							
7:00	102⁸ 96-60 124-16		3:00 112-80 84-80	64	102³ 88-52 64-12		73	50	34	25	182
				65							
6:57	104/₁₀₂ 84-56 72-24		2:53 96-68 88-48	67	102⁸/₉₉ 72-44 76-12		77	51	74	25	227
6:54	84-52 76-40		2:47 96-60 100-76	68	– 76-44 88-24		77	60	74	10	221
7:04	103⁴/₁₀₀ 96-60 104-40	Novice Rider.		70							
6:59	104⁵/₁₀₁ 92-52 96-32		3:02 80-60 88-60	71	101⁸ 60-52 80-16	–2	85	57	74	25	239
...ed				72							
7:00	101³ 72-52 136-44		2:57 144-64 96-108	73	101⁸ 64-44 96-40		79	59	72	25	235
6:59	102³ 76-48 70-28		2:55 92-68 76-88	74	101³ 74-52 104-52		79	57	82	25	243
condition – Did not start.				76							

AND INTERESTED PEOPLE AFTER THE RIDE

Bibliography

Academic Division, Cavalry School. *Animal Management*. Fort Riley, Kansas, 1926.

Adams, O. R. *Lameness in Horses*. Philadelphia: Lea and Febiger, 1966.

Bolton, Lyndon. *Training the Horse*. New York: October House, 1964.

British Horse Society. *The Manual of Horsemanship*. London: The British Horse Society, 1964.

Brown, William Robinson. *The Horse of the Desert*. Springville, N.Y.: Jay Shuler Co., 1967.

Butler, Doug. *The Principles of Horseshoeing*. Ithaca: Doug Butler, 1974.

Carter, Col. W. H. *Horses, Saddles and Bridles*. Baltimore: Lord Baltimore Press, 1902.

Chenevix-Trench, Charles. *A History of Horsemanship*. Garden City, N.Y.: Doubleday and Co., 1970.

Codrington, Lt.-Col. W. S. *Know Your Horse. A Guide to Selection and Care in Health and Disease*. London: J. A. Allen and Co., 1975.

Collins, Lt.-Col. W. Lyon. *First Aid Hints for the Horse Owner*. London: St. James's Place, 1972.

Conn, Dr. George. *Treating Common Diseases of Your Horse*. Hollywood, Calif.: Wilshire Book Co., 1974.

Darwin, Charles. *The Expression of the Emotions in Man and Animals*. Chicago: University of Chicago Press, 1970.

Davidson, Joseph. *Horsemen's Veterinary Adviser*. Del-Jay Products, Cleveland, Ohio.

Denning, Dr. Charles H. *First Aid for Horses*. Hollywood, Calif.: Wilshire Book Co., 1974.

Edwards, Gladys Brown. *Anatomy and Conformation of the Horse*. Croton-on-Hudson, New York: Dreenan Press, 1973.

Ensminger, M. E. *Horses and Horsemanship*. Danville, Illinois: Interstate Printers and Publishers, 1956.

Fillis, James. *Breaking and Riding with Military Commentaries*. London: Hurst and Blackett.

Goubaux, Armand, and Barrier, Gustave. *Exterior of the Horse*. Philadelphia: Lippincott and Co., 1904.

Hayes, Captain Horace. *Stable Management and Exercise*. London: J. A. Allen and Co., 1965.

————. *Points of the Horse*. New York: Arco Publishing Co., 1969.

————. *Veterinary Notes for Horse Owners*. New York: Arco Publishing Co., 1965.

Hediger, H. *Psychology and Behavior of Animals in Zoos and Circuses*. New York: Dover Publications, 1968.

Holmes, Charles. *Principles and Practice of Horse Shoeing*. Leeds, England: Ferriers Journal Publishing Co., 1949.

Hyland, Ann. *Beginners Guide to Endurance Riding*. London: Pelham Books, 1975.

Jankovich, Miklos. *They Rode into Europe*. London: Harrap and Co., 1971.

Jones, Dr. William. *Locomotion and Lameness*. Fort Collins, Colo.: Caballus Publishers, 1975.

Jones, William, and Bogart, Ralph. *Genetics of the Horse*. Ann Arbor, Mich.: Edwards Brothers, 1971.

Kays, D. J. *The Horse*. Cranbury, N.J.: A. S. Barnes and Co., 1969.

Littauer, Captain Vladimir. *Schooling Your Horse*. Princeton, N.J.: Van Nostrand Co., 1956.

————. *Horseman's Progress. Development of Modern Riding*. Princeton, N.J.: Van Nostrand Co. n.d.

Manwell, Marion C. *How to Shoe a Horse*. Cranbury, N.J.: A. S. Barnes and Co., 1968.

Marshall, Major F. C. *Elements of Hippology. Prepared for the Department of Tactics, United States Military Academy*. Kansas City: Franklin Hudson Co., 1925.

Mohr, Dr. Erna. *The Asiatic Wild Horse*. London: J. A. Allen and Co., 1971.

Paillard, St. Fort, Jean. *Understanding Equitation*. New York: Doubleday and Co., 1974.

Robert, Tom. *Horse Control and the Bit*. Northern Argus, Clare, South Australia: Tilbrook Brothers, 1971.

Rogers, Tex. *Mare Owners Handbook*. Houston: Cordovan Corporation, 1971.

Rooney, James. *The Lame Horse*. Cranbury, N.J.: A. S. Barnes and Co., 1974.

Sidney, S. *Illustrated Book of the Horse*. Hollywood, Calif.: Wilshire Book Co., 1974.

Smyth, R. H. *The Mind of the Horse*. London: J. A. Allen and Co., 1965.

Steffen, Randy. *U.S. Military Saddles*. Norman, Okla.: University of Oklahoma Press, 1973.

Summerhays, Reginald. *The Arabian Horse*. Hollywood, Calif.: Wilshire Publishing Co., 1969.

Taylor, Louis. *Bits. Their Use and Misuse.* New York: Harper and Row, 1966.
Vernam, Glenn. *Man on Horseback.* Lincoln, Neb.: University of Nebraska Press, Bison Books, 1972.
Wagoner, Don. (Ed.) *Conditioning to Win.* Grapevine, Tex.: Equine Research Publications, 1974.
Willett, Peter. *The Thoroughbred.* London: Weidenfeld and Nicolson, 1970.
Westbrook, Ann and Perry. *Trail Horses and Trail Riding.* Hollywood, Calif.: Wilshire Book Co., 1972.
Williams, Moyra. *Practical Horse Psychology.* Hollywood, Calif.: Wilshire Book Co., 1973.
Wynmalen, Henry. *Horse Breeding and Stud Management.* London: Country Life, Ltd., 1950.

MANUALS AND PAMPHLETS

Veterinary Technicians. Department of the Army Technical Manual, August 1951.
A Manual of Equitation. Academic Division, The Cavalry School, Fort Riley, Kansas, 1927.
Care of Animals. Training Regulations prepared under direction of the Chief of Cavalry, Washington, D.C., 1927.
Principles of Horse Feeding. U.S. Department of Agriculture, Washington, D.C., 1903.
Trail Riding. International Arabian Horse Association, Burbank, California.
Endurance Riding. International Arabian Horse Association, Burbank, California.
Proceedings of the Twentieth Annual Convention of the American Association of Equine Practitioners, Las Vegas, Nevada, 1974.
Distance Riding Manual, Appaloosa Horse Club, Moscow, Idaho, 1973.
Endurance and Competitive Trail Riding Manual, prepared by Wentworth and Linda Tellington, Pacific Coast Equestrian Research Farm, Badger, California, 1967.
1974 Yearbook of Endurance Riding. American Endurance Ride Conference, Auburn, California.

MAGAZINES

Stable Management. Chislehurst, Kent, England
The Morgan Horse. New York, N.Y.
The Cavalry Journal. Out of Print
Journal of the American Veterinary Medical Association. Chicago, Ill.
The Appaloosa News. Moscow, Idaho

Practical Horseman. West Chester, Penna.
The Chronicle of the Horse. Middleburg, Va.
Western Horseman. Colorado Springs, Col.
Saddle Action. Paso Robles, Calif.
Horse and Rider. Temecula, Calif.
Horse and Horseman. Capistrano Beach, Calif.
American Quarter Horse Assn. Amarillo, Texas
Northeast Horseman. Hampden Highlands, Maine

Index